Our God Wears Denim Overalls

Our God Wears
Denim Overalls

Glenn H. Goree

FOREWORDS BY
Lesley Tonkin Allan
Richard Amiss
AND Jenni Searle

RESOURCE *Publications* · Eugene, Oregon

OUR GOD WEARS DENIM OVERALLS

Resource Publications
An Imprint of Wipf and Stock Publishers
199 W. 8th Ave., Suite 3
Eugene, OR 97401

www.wipfandstock.com

PAPERBACK ISBN: 978-1-5326-3946-3
HARDCOVER ISBN: 978-1-5326-3947-0
EBOOK ISBN: 978-1-5326-3948-7

Manufactured in the U.S.A.

This book is dedicated to

Gwendoline Maud Massey
July 26, 1920–July 22, 2017

Matriarch, foundation, and cornerstone of our family.
She will be missed.
We look forward to joining her one day in Jesus's presence.

Contents

Foreword

Lesley Tonkin Allan

It is a pleasure to write this foreword for Glenn, a former colleague and friend of over thirty years. We worked for the Rhodesian operation of Africa's largest retailer and manufacturer, during a time when relationships and trust were fractured by the civil war Glenn mentions. Our personal security was threatened at times and we got to appreciate first-hand the phrase, *"one man's terrorist is another's freedom fighter"*.

As I read *Our God Wears Denim Overalls*, I imagined Glenn speaking in his likeable Texan drawl (which had initially sounded so strange to our insular Central African ears). I felt acutely aware of his physical presence. And what a presence it was! Well over 6 feet tall, broad-shouldered and muscular with slightly wavy dark brown hair, the description, "tall, dark and handsome" was fitting. We aptly nicknamed Glenn, "Clark Kent", who, as you will know, was Superman's disguise, enabling him to mix with ordinary people. It seemed particularly fitting then that the key focus of Glenn's book is about God stripping himself of all privileges and dignity and becoming human.

In New Zealand (one of the most secular countries in the world) the idea of God as an ordinary person *"wearing denim overalls"* would likely be met with *"Yeah, right!"* (The typical 'Kiwi' response to a statement totally lacking credibility.) However, no matter how cynical these readers might be, they would be curious enough to find out more about the wearer of those overalls. Glenn's depiction of Jesus as a loving, protective parent, compassionate, supportive and intimately concerned for our wellbeing would be surprising. For so many, God is stern and disapproving, quick to judge, remote and aloof.

Like Superman, Glenn is grounded by strong, moral principles, and also used his many abilities for good in different environments, military and civilian, religious and secular. Accepting of others and sensitive to cultural nuances, he had the gift of quickly establishing rapport and being at ease with people whether they were on the mission field or in a sophisticated fashion retail store. We knew him as a man with good values and a deep faith. God blessed him with a good sense of humour which was fortunate, as he was frequently the butt of friendly ribbing. Life and work experiences have tested his faith. Having walked in the shoes of others, he writes sincerely, from a heart which feels what others feel and experiences which others have experienced.

Why would God, described by Glenn as someone whose "arms . . . embraced the universe, hands that held creation and feet that crossed the Milky Way", set aside all the privileges and advantages of deity and become human? And why, "when the going got tough" did he not claim any special privilege? He remained, as Jesus, humble and obedient to death—on a crucifix!

Glenn's writing has prompted me to search deep inside myself for answers to this question.

I believe that Jesus, my companion on life's journey, sets an example. He chose not to remain in heaven, but to be part of a broken world full of desperation and destruction, (and delight). With compassionate care, he tended to the needs of the poor, the hungry, the sinners and outcasts of society. He made himself unpopular in exposing injustice and its causes. He empowered the weak and restored their dignity and value as human beings.

My life has to be modelled on that of Jesus. When measured against him, how well do I do? How well would you do?

The challenge for me is to serve without expectations. I end with my favourite prayer, learned as a child but only fully understood and appreciated as a mature adult.

"Teach us, good Lord, to serve you as you deserve; to give and not to count the cost; to fight and not to heed the wounds; to toil and not to seek for rest; to labour and not to ask for any reward, save that of knowing that we do your will."

St. Ignatius Loyola

Lesley Tonkin Allan

Foreword

Richard Amiss

It is inherent in human nature to ask questions, and I believe many people ponder what it would be like if Jesus's first coming had been to our present-day world. The pinnacle reason I believe we can even get a grasp on what God is like is to use the familiar to describe Him. Jesus walking in sandals, sweating, and bleeding are things we all do. While we may ask questions, we are also reminded by Glenn in this book that Jesus is much more familiar with us than we are with him. If Jesus came into our present world, He would put his brilliant crown down and would continue to relate to us on our level. Everyone can identify with blue jeans. Blue jeans have a way of evening the playing field.

God is aware that we have a limited understanding and can only absorb a finite amount of information. In His ocean of mercy, Jesus *dumbs it down* for us, providing what we can handle without being overwhelmed. Jesus takes tremendous care by meeting us where we are, and we then have the choice of trusting or not trusting.

We may search our lives to find Jesus or to reveal ultimate truths, but the Bible teaches us to trust and to believe what our eyes cannot see. Glenn points out that our Creator, who is beyond description, understands us and can make Himself like us so we can understand.

Glenn poses many interesting questions that I bet each of us has asked at some time. What is it like in heaven? What do angels hear? Why did Jesus come to earth knowing death on the cross awaited him? Reading this book reminds us that it is okay to wonder, to question, to use our minds, because these actions help us to be more in tune with our own paths. Each of us has a path, a mission to be the unique person God made us to be. We can question God with humility, and there is nothing wrong in wondering like a child. What we may find is that what we are looking for is not somewhere out there, but it is within each of us already.

Farmers work hard, sunup to sundown, unnoticed most of the time. Isn't it the same way with Jesus? Most of what He is doing we are not even aware of. He reminded people that He was doing His Father's work when He was on earth, and today we can find that He is still busy doing his Father's work.

Thank God we can ask questions but still not have all the answers. Because, don't you know, if we knew everything, we would try to take control. And what a disaster that would be! Instead, we are encouraged to trust and to put everything in Jesus's big, strong hands. Or we can doubt, which we are all usually better at doing.

Glenn's book reminds us to wait on Jesus, ask as many questions as we want, and if we need God to be a farmer if He were here in the present day, then so be it. Many times I have just wanted to sit with Jesus personally and have a frank discussion without all the ceremony. I believe Glenn is trying to bring Jesus down to earth, to portray Him as a regular guy we can relate to, knowing that He is both man and God.

Our job is to love God, love ourselves, and love our neighbors. Anything other than that is to diminish life. Glenn is keeping his eyes on Jesus and he is not looking behind or in front of Him. Like the tree no one wanted had a mission to fulfill, we need to find that mission within ourselves. When we love ourselves, Jesus is exemplified more because we have no identity apart from Him. The Great I Am can show up anyway He wants to, and He does, often in a pair of blue jeans.

Richard Amiss, D Min., RPT-S, LPC-S

Clinical Education Program Coordinator
Doctor of Ministry in Christian Counseling
Registered Play Therapist-Supervisor
Licensed Professional Counselor-Supervisor
The Ecumenical Center for Education, Counseling and Health
8310 Ewing Halsell Dr.
San Antonio, TX 78229

Foreword

Jenni Searle

L ittle did I know way back in the late seventies, early eighties
when, in my capacity as Human Resources Officer for the
then Rhodesian sector of Africa's largest retail and manufacturing
organisation, that the man I interviewed and recommended for
the available position would become a long-standing friend who
would have a major impact on my life.

That man was Glenn Goree—born and bred in Texas, USA,
living in Rhodesia later to become Zimbabwe, during a very difficult period in the history of our beautiful nation. Glenn alludes
to some of those difficulties and challenges in his book. Many of
those difficulties and challenges still exist, and in some ways have
intensified, but as Glenn writes 'strength demonstrated while suffering persecution is infectious'. The presence of God Almighty
sustains and teaches us to live by faith and not by sight.

Our God Wears Denim Overalls is such a refreshing picture
of the reality of Who Jesus actually is. Whatever I need Him to be,
whenever I need Him to be it, that's Who He is. Glenn's delight-
ful descriptions of Jesus rising before the sun, labouring until full
moon, working in the fields of lost souls, rolling up His sleeves
and dealing with the enemy, gathering to Himself all those who
respond to His call just bring so much joy to my heart as I consider
all that Jesus has done and continues to do in our nation of Zimbabwe and in my life as an individual.

Earlier I mentioned that Glenn has had a major impact on my
life. The God that Glenn speaks of and describes so beautifully in

his book, has birthed in our troubled land of Zimbabwe a ministry that is positioned by God to lead His people back to His unfailing love, back to a place of personal healing, wholeness and restoration. More than thirty years later Glenn and his wife Valerie have been instrumental in contributing to the success of this ministry.

During our time together as friends and colleagues, I have seen in Glenn a man who is firmly grounded in the truth of God's Word, living out his Christian principles in his home, in the work place, in fact in every area of his life. I humbly submit that Glenn's experiences over the years, many of which are described in this book, coupled with his knowledge of the Scriptures and his obvious love of our Lord and Saviour, have prepared him to write this book. Our God Wears Denim Overalls is a true story of how much God the Father, God the Son, and God the Holy Spirit love us and the lengths He went to in order to rescue us from our sin and from the enemy. This profound truth is put across in such a way that the reader should be challenged to the very core of his/her being—we should all ask ourselves the question 'what did I ever do to deserve such favour?' The answer to that of course is that we can do nothing to change the way God loves us. His love is unfailing, never ending and completely unconditional, and His grace is sufficient for us.

As you read Glenn's book, let that love flow over you, know that whatever situation you find yourself in, there is a way out and His Name is Jesus! He understands, He has been where you are. Let the truth of God's Word set out so beautifully in the stories that follow bring you to your knees in worship and adoration of the King of Kings and the Lord of Lords. (John 8 vs. 32: Jesus said: 'If you hold to my teaching, you are really my disciples. Then you will know the truth and the truth will set you free.')

Jenni Searle

Founding Director:
Life in the Light Ministries:
Bulawayo Zimbabwe

Introduction

What is your image of Jesus? Do you see him as he is depicted in most paintings? Long, flowing, dark brown hair, with expertly set waves that could only come from the most expensive beauty salon. Look closely at his peaches-and-cream complexion. Not a pockmark or blemish in sight. His countenance glows bright enough to cast a shadow on the sun, and he appears to have emerged from a bath of cow's milk taken from only the purest bovine.

Women would sacrifice their first born to have his eyes, eyelashes, and thick, luscious lips. Eyebrows plucked to perfection, no crows feet, no wrinkles, but perfect contours and symmetry. Ah, beauty like no one has ever seen.

Next, if you examine paintings of his hands, they can only be described as soft as goose down or lamb's wool, and as pallid as a newborn babe.

There are no physical descriptions of Jesus recorded in the Bible. However, you'd think artist read these verses from the Song of Solomon and applied them to the Son of God.

"Your neck is like the tower of David, built with elegance; on it hang a thousand shields, all of them shields of warriors." (Song of Songs 4:4)

> "Your neck is like an ivory tower. Your eyes are the pools of Heshbon by the gate of Bath Rabbim. Your nose is like the tower of Lebanon looking toward Damascus. Your head crowns you like Mount Carmel. Your hair is like royal tapestry; the king is held captive by its tresses. How

beautiful you are and how pleasing, O love, with your delights!" (Song of Songs 7:4–6)

The irony of the situation is that these verses were describing a woman and not a man!

Why have artists, for the last 2000 years, misrepresented the physical appearance of Jesus? Do they assume a different portrayal would be sacrilegious? I often wonder how many unbelievers have seen this weak, defenseless, and misleading representation of the person of Christ, and allowed it to color their perception of him? So affected by the portrayal of Jesus as a delicate flower that they are repulsed by what they see? How can they be positively influenced by a milquetoast shadow of a man?

In my counseling practice, I have had the displeasure of listening to men say, "If that's what Jesus looked like, I want no part of him." When questioned, these men admitted that their only exposure to Jesus the Man was in poorly represented images they'd seen in paintings, stained-glass church windows, and Christian literature.

Isn't it sad that a person's soul could be won or lost by a single pictorial misrepresentation?

Since these antagonists chose to be blinded by their own preconceived biases and prejudices of Jesus the Man, they stopped cold turkey learning about Jesus the Savior. No matter how many times I tried to explain that these various art forms were misrepresentations, these men had already drawn their own conclusions. Their preconceptions and predispositions were permanently set, just like cement blocks after drying outdoors under the hot summer sun.

This unfortunate situation begs several important questions. How do we reconcile Jesus the Man with Jesus the Savior? How does any discerning Bible student square the dark-skinned, single Hebrew male, baked in the Judean sun with the Messiah the son of God? And finally, how does a person who wants an objective inquiry reconcile Jesus the carpenter covered with cuts and bruises, and calloused hands with the resurrected Savior? We will find answers in the book of Hebrews.

"Since the children have flesh and blood, he too shared in their humanity so that by his death he might destroy him who holds the power of death—that is, the devil—and free those who all their lives were held in slavery by their fear of death. For surely it is not angels he helps, but Abraham's descendants. For this reason, he had to be made like his brothers in every way, in order that he might become a merciful and faithful high priest in service to God, and that he might make atonement for the sins of the people. Because he himself suffered when he was tempted, he is able to help those who are being tempted." (Heb. 2:14–18)

What does it mean that Jesus was like us in every way? This question has been addressed many times in sermons, and books written by scholars who are more academically astute than I. So, what can I have to offer that is different from the discourse already in print?

Here is my supposition. I believe that if our Lord and Savior lived in today's world, he would wear blue denim overalls! I think he would feel uncomfortable in a suit and tie, making a living in an office as a white-collar professional.

You may be thinking there's just something unholy about saying Jesus would wear blue denim. It's not only unholy, it's blasphemous, irreverent, and sacrilegious. Some people may say the suggestion almost seems to communicate wearing blue cotton denim overalls is beneath his station as God. After all, is Jesus not the Savior? Is he not the redeemer? Was he not raised on the third day after his death on the cross? Didn't he defeat death and Satan? Dressed in such garb is insulting to his mission to die on the cross, and a desecration to his royal seat next to God.

But that is precisely the point.

Imagining Jesus in overalls is also earthy, mortal, fleshy, and . . . well, human.

Who else but carpenters, farmers, and ranchers wearing cotton denim overalls know the sting of salty sweat in their eyes under the hot sun? Who else but a skilled worker wearing overalls knows what it means to live a Spartan life?

For example, I never realized how heavy hay bales were until I helped load them one summer day in the southwest Texas heat. I was worn out before noon because I hadn't learnt the technique of flipping those bales by leverage and not by using raw muscle and sinew.

I believe if Jesus were born in the 21st century, his earthy father would have been a farmer, plumber, mechanic, or some other artisan or tradesman. Jesus would have had several pairs of cotton bibs—one for work, one for wearing around the house, and one for special occasions. He would have been raised in a home where he was up before the sun, and in bed long after it set, working six days a week. And I don't mean nine to five either. Jesus would be up before the rooster crowed, and in bed long after the birds settled in for the night on the telephone line outside his bedroom window.

Long before his thirtieth birthday, he would have had callused hands, any number of scars all over his limbs, busted knuckles, a broken finger or two, missing fingernails, scraped knees, and swollen elbows. Not to mention a constant array of cuts and bruises.

More than likely Jesus would not have long, flowing hair. It would probably be cut short, in a burr. But if he did grow it long, he would have put it up in a ponytail while he worked or covered it by his baseball cap. He would have received a couple of bumps on his head from banging it against metal engines on tractors, trucks, or cars. Grease? He would know what it's like to end a day by rinsing his hands and arms in gasoline before he could wash them with Lava soap. I think he wouldn't complain about the pain in his back and neck from being under a vehicle all day while working on the chassis above him.

I believe Jesus would have the proverbial farmer's tan. His arms, neck, and face would be dark brown from being in the sun all day. But, when he went swimming in the local pond or lake, his untanned torso and legs would stick out like a newborn baby's skin. The next day he would be fishing in the same body of water.

As a robust youth, he probably broke at least an arm or a leg falling out of a tree, and how often would he have roamed the hills and fields near his house? Hunting and camping would have been a big part of his life, and he may have even been a Boy Scout.

We could go on and on about how ordinary he was, and how he led a similar life to his peers, all in preparation for one task—to be our Savior.

In the following chapters we are going to explore Christ as an ordinary man. We will allow the Scriptures to tell us about his sunburned face, sweat-stung eyes, powerful arms, muscular back, gnarled but gentle hands, and dusty, aching feet. It is my hope that as we indulge in this exploration of Jesus the Man, we will emerge with a deeper faith in Jesus the Savior.

1

Our God Wears Denim Overalls

Our God wears blue cotton denim overalls,
Faded and threadbare from responding to His vocational call.

He rises before the sun, and labors until full moon.
His only break is when He blesses a crust around high noon.

Sweat is His sole companion, stinging the corner of His eyes,
And at day's end, a bed of straw or hay is where He usually lies.

The fields in which He devotes His life are not of corn or maize,
Nor does He drive a combine under the sun's blistering haze.

No, His fields are souls whose lives are lost in this life's mortal sin,
He worries because after their death, He knows they can't begin again.

So, He rolls up his sleeves, bearing sunburned, muscled arms,
And He exposes Satan's lies who deceives with insidious charms.

Then He gathers from the fields those who respond to His call,
Giving each one a home in a garden from which they can never fall.

The sun flamed from its lofty royal palace in the heavens, forcing all living, breathing organisms exposed to its radiance to seek shade or at least a drop of moisture for their dehydrated cracked lips. If good fortune blessed them, they may be able to swish around a mouthful of water and relieve a parched tongue.

Man, fowl, or four-legged beast all had one goal at this time of day—stay out of the open and find sanctuary for the next several hours. The power of the sun cannot be beaten. There were mile-high piles of dried bones, man and beast alike, who had disregarded this rule of nature.

But only man challenges the odds of surviving amidst the scorching armada of the sun's rays. These rays have only one goal—to envelop any and all with the glory of their mother sun's brilliance. No warning is needed and no quarter will be given to those who test her daylight campaign. In moderation, warmth is appreciated, but in excess, it can become lethal when her fiery ambassadors rain a fury of fire no flesh can indefinitely endure.

What benefits a man who shakes his fist at the sun? Nothing, because he has to earn a living. Therefore, he rises before the light of the morning star, and works in the elements until the evening star. Only he will toil when all other creatures take refuge from the deadly heat. Defiantly, he will wipe away the stinging sweat from the corners of his eyes. Boldly, only mankind will labor in his cotton overalls planting crops, repairing motors, mending fences, harvesting wheat or corn, or constructing buildings.

Tired cannot describe how he feels at day's end. Fatigue only begins to express his aching muscles, sore feet, scared hands, and throbbing back. Don't forget about the scrapes and cuts where flesh and bone lost their quarrel with iron or steel. Then at day's end, he is too tired to sleep and tosses and turns. This nocturnal habit usually wakes and irritates his wife until she boots him out of the bed. The living room couch becomes his refuge. Yes, he's tired but he is also preoccupied with what needs to be done tomorrow. Work is like the rainy season, there is never enough rain to fully soak the earth, and there are never enough hours in the day to get the work done.

Days seem to blur into weeks, weeks into months, and months into years. Watches? Who needs them? Just look up in the sky at the position of the sun. Maybe its location isn't entirely accurate to the minute, but he can estimate how much daylight is left. No other time-monitoring instruments are required because time is best gauged by what still needs to be done before the sun sets.

At some point, work became a calling, rooted in pride, promise, and wellbeing. Each task, each small act became an investment in something larger than himself. It was as though everything he did was not for him, but for those he loved, those he cared for, and those he cherished. Then, he grasped the reality that his labor was no longer only about his immediate family, but about the other folk his work impacted. The work of his hands had a ripple affect that impacted his community, his country, and in fact, the whole world. He reasoned that the quality of his work and the message it carried reached untold numbers of people.

If he were a farmer, each row he carefully tilled would touch the thousands of people his crops fed. The more introspective he became, the more productive his fields. If he were a mechanic, each nut and bolt replaced in its proper position with just the right torque touched lives. The quality of his work could mean the difference between life and death. If he were a plumber, each pipe he positioned and each fixture he assembled impacted thousands of lives. After all, was he not orchestrating the use of one of earth's most valuable resources so it was distributed more efficiently?

These blue-collar professionals represent all hard-working men and women who answer to a higher calling, bigger and more noble than themselves. Every person laboring feels like they are part of a grander scheme which, in turn, makes them take greater pride in their work.

I know I may have used poetic license as this is not exactly what goes through their minds each day. But if I were to put their work ethic into words, this is how I would describe it. Besides, when I was working my way through college, I met some of these skilled men. They took pride in their skills and spoke of them almost in religious terms. Could this explain why they were always busy even during difficult financial times?

To me, this is not mere poetic license, but part of my life-experience. In the early years of our marriage, mid-70s, my wife and I lived among farmers and a ranching community while we worked on a mission station in Rhodesia, now Zimbabwe. Due to our close proximity, I was able to rub elbows with them on a weekly basis. Their way of living and the pride they displayed in their skills reminded me of the workmen I encountered while earning money for college during the summer months.

However, these men in Rhodesia did not wear cotton denim overalls. Their daily attire consisted of khaki shorts, short-sleeved cotton shirts, knee-socks, soft leather shoes they called *veldskoene*, and floppy canvas hats. Year-round they usually wore short sleeved shirts, even in winter. You see, due to the elevation and being in the tropics, nights and early mornings were cold, but once the sun came up, sweaters or jackets were no longer needed. Hence, most farmers and ranchers ignored the initial morning cold and warmed up by physically working hard.

We met some of these men and women who homesteaded the land after World War II. They started with nothing more than a dream and very little money. Thirty years later, in the 1970s, they were prosperous tobacco or maize farmers, and cattle ranchers. There were no home-improvement DIY stores so they learned to be mechanics, electricians, masons, architects, builders, plumbers, and whatever else they had to do to survive. There was a time when there was no electricity supply to the outlying area so many home-owners used their own generators. Water was not piped in by the local authorities because there was no municipality close by. They drilled their own wells and dug their own stock tanks.

As you may understand, day to day survival without the amenities most people take for granted was a struggle, not to mention the business of farming and ranching. All of the above depiction can be compared to the pioneer days of American history. However, there was one hardship that was unique to these farmers and ranchers in Rhodesia—protection against baboons.

Troops of baboons were a problem because they frequently raided the corn fields. So add another job to the endless list—hunter. The weary farmer had to learn how to track his quarry like Davy Crocket or Daniel Boone. Now, the average American reading this may think that baboons can't be much of a problem. After all, we see them in zoos and they are fun to watch. However, in the wild, even leopards give them a wide berth as they are formidable and deadly adversaries. Their sharp teeth can tear flesh from bone, and their group mentality endows them with fearlessness.

Work ethic comes in all shapes and sizes. The headmaster of the secondary school lived in a thatched-roof home on the mission compound. One bitterly cold night, his house caught on fire, started by sparks from his chimney. The house burned to the ground because there was no water to fight the fire. The mission had water pumped from a river to a tank on a hill which provided each house with an in-door supply, but the water pressure was minimal. We staff and students did our best to save the family's furniture, clothing, and other possessions by rescuing items until the flames became too fierce. Then we formed a bucket brigade from the closest outside faucet to the house.

Although we didn't save the house, I want to emphasis the faith of this community of students and teachers. In their faith I saw the face of Jesus. In their faith I saw his sacrifice on the cross. In their Christian commitment I saw the Father and Holy Spirit at work in their lives. They did not wear the cross as a piece of jewelry, instead they bore his cross every day. In their lives I saw the burden shared.

Each time a whip hit Jesus's back they felt it tear into their flesh. When nails were driven into his hands they felt the iron spike drive between the bones of their wrists. As he hung on the cross gasping for breath it was their lungs that were collapsing. It was also their blood streaming into their eyes from the thorns spiked into their foreheads from his crown. Their mouths were parched and they begged for water only to be given vinegar. Then, when their bodies could take torture no longer, they cried out with Jesus, "It is finished!" (John 19:30)

Some people reading my comparison of these people's lives to Christ's struggles on earth may think it's over the top, even blasphemous. But when we hear sermons about bearing Jesus's Cross, it seems to me the mission community lived the perfect example.

Here is another series of events that exemplify a living faith.

In early 1976, we held a series of worship services in the community clubhouse about 25 miles from the mission. The theme during the five consecutive Sundays was to ask God to deliver Rhodesia from the terrorist war. Terrorists had infiltrated our sector which made daily life a gamble. When husbands and wives said good-bye at the beginning of each day they didn't know if they would see each other again that night. This rural community consisted of hundreds of miles with only dirt roads, and the nearest town of any size boasted only a gas station, post office, and small hotel. The local area clubhouse was a focal point for the community where people could gather for parties, meetings, or just relaxing.

By this time, the terrorist war had been raging for seven years. Local families lived with the weight of never knowing if or when a group of terrorists was going to ambush them. This constant threat proved to be a heavy burden for everyone. Attending church services became a hazardous gamble. How could they know if landmines had been placed in the road after the terrorists recognized their pattern each Sunday? What about the fear of a terrorist ambush as the family vehicle rounded a bend in the road, or approached the crest of a hill?

Unlike contemporary church-goers in western society, these farmers and ranchers were taking calculated risks when they traveled to worship Jesus. They knew that when they left their homes in the morning there was a strong possibility that they might not return later in the day.

The terrorists ruled by night and the farmers by day. The enemy wore no uniforms but donned civilian clothing to blend in with the local population and farm workers. This guerilla tactic allowed them to reconnoiter the traffic patterns of the civilians, police, military, and paramilitary. A terrorist could be someone from whom you asked directions, or a man you hired to work on your ranch or farm. No amount of security could overcome the presence of the enemy hiding in plain sight.

As I look back on those weeks, I'm tempted to chuckle at the sight at the front door each Sunday morning, but I don't laugh because of the seriousness of the situation. As the people entered the clubhouse, they left their weapons and supporting ammunition stacked in the foyer. The collection looked like an arsenal for the United States Marines. There were shotguns, pistols, Uzis, various calibers of hunting rifles, all manner of weapons except hand grenades. People who had those devices left them in their vehicles. And covering the coatrack were a variety of ammunition belts.

And yet, in spite of the risks, families came each Sunday. No one complained. They all acted like it was a typical Sunday picnic in a peaceful community.

When I reflect on these farmers and ranchers thirty-two years later, several thoughts come to mind.

First, this was a community of Christians. The people were from several different faiths such as Roman Catholic, Anglican, and Protestant, but all present gathered as one body. Our worship consisted of song, Scripture, and prayer, with our focus on Jesus.

Second, I think of their sacrifice. When I was growing up in Texas I heard many excuses for people not to attend services on a Sunday morning. For example, the building was too hot or too cold, or someone disliked the color of the curtains or carpet, or felt the pews were uncomfortable. Maybe others thought the preacher was too long-winded, or didn't like him personally. What about when a visitor chose to sit in *their* seats? Oh, I almost forgot— Sunday National Football League games! If church services started earlier, I wouldn't miss the kick-off.

Third, I think of their example. I don't know of another time in my life when traveling to attend worship was so fraught with potential danger, where fear of death was involved just in the journey. This is the closest I've been to what I imagine the first century Christians experienced.

You may find this next phrase histrionic, but I miss it! I miss the adrenaline rush from the apprehension of not knowing once I left my home that I might not make it to worship because of a land mine or terrorist ambush. And then, after the worship service, I again would be at risk in my return trip home.

I miss knowing that in spite of the risk, I had a faithful wife who never blinked an eye. She was always there to support, guide, and correct. I miss being in danger because of sharing our faith with others. I miss knowing that although our lives were on the line, Jesus was right there with us. I miss knowing that we were sharing this small blip of an historic moment with fellow Christians who were doing the same.

It was exciting, almost intoxicating, to know in a small way we were part of something more important than ourselves. It was thrilling to be able to share this human reach for what was far above our human imperfections.

Fourth, I think of their strength. Were we afraid? I would answer this question three-fold. First, my wife and I were both too young and inexperienced in life and too idealistic to know we should have been afraid. Second, when it dawned on us that we should be afraid, it was usually after the fact. Third, our community was living with this threat before we arrived and would continue long after we left the mission. What we experienced was nothing. Unlike us, they could not leave. This was their home.

You may think what I just described was youthful inexperience, and it probably was. However, it was this community's strength to carry on no matter what may happen that, through Christ, gave my wife and I our strength. When I ponder the depth of their faith, I am reminded of the last two thousand years of Christianity. This farming community, like Christians throughout the centuries, proved that strength demonstrated while suffering persecution is infectious.

Fifth, there was an outpouring of love. I knew it was a tight-knit community. They had to be closely involved, like an extended family, so they could survive both as farmers and ranchers, as well as defenders of their way of life. I noticed something more. There was charity, compassion, and support. Grievances and pettiness were overlooked and forgiven. I think for my wife and me personally as *outsiders* and Americans, they showered us with kindness and acceptance beyond what we expected or deserved.

Sixth, we had a taste of heaven. We experienced living for something superior to ourselves. We were also blessed to share this Christian ideal with brethren in Christ of all faiths. This opportunity to serve opened a window into heaven. Briefly, if only for a moment, we tasted heaven. We sat at Christ's table and enjoyed a feast of holiness that can only come from God. The spiritual food was a feast that did not fill my heart, but made me hungry for more.

Seventh, some gave the ultimate sacrifice. During the two years we were on the mission two farmers were attacked, but no one was seriously injured or killed. After we left the area, two farmers were murdered on their own property. One had a landmine planted in his dirt driveway overnight, and he was killed early the next morning. The other man was ambushed in one of his own fields and beaten to death with rocks, clubs, and probably the butt of an AK 47. To me personally, these two men were examples of Christians who put their faith in God and were willing to follow him all the way. As in all wars, in spite of how strong a faith someone may have, there is no guarantee that faith will stop a bullet.

So what does this story have to do with Jesus being our God who wore cotton denim overalls?

Everything.

During the time Jesus lived on the earth, nearly everyone was either directly or indirectly connected to agriculture. Some people may have only had a small garden, but at least part of their food supply came from their own hand. I learned to love and respect the farmers in the rural area surrounding the mission in Rhodesia. They were self-reliant, much in the same way farmers would have been in the time of Christ. People in both groups had to be a jack-of-all-trades and master of none in order to keep their homesteads financially viable. The farmers of these two different historical periods and from diverse parts of the world had other traits in common. They both lived in changing times in violent worlds. Just like the Jews 2000 years ago never knew when Roman soldiers would sweep into Judea, my farming neighbors never knew when they would be ambushed and murdered by communist terrorists.

Jesus often featured farmers in the parables he taught. Why? Because, like the farmer, he too was a common man. As a carpenter of his day, he would have worn the *denim overalls* of his time. Jesus, like the blue-collar worker today, was born of the earth and connected to the soil. After all, did he not begin his life at birth in a stable? His work was hard, backbreaking, and time consuming.

Sweat stung the corners of his eyes, dripped from his forehead, and he probable had splinters too numerous to count. By the time he was thirty, thick callouses had developed on both hands.

Although Jesus was not a farmer, his connection to hard, physical labor gave credence to his use of farming analogies to express his concern for souls. In his mind, every field was symbolic of the many people in pain who needed the help only his Father could offer. The fields of crops to be harvested were endless, like the lost souls of earth. These were good people, harmless, wanting someone to guide them. Jesus was their answer because he began his life, not as God, but as a peasant.

Now, I ask you to stop reading this book for a moment. Open your Bible and turn to Matthew chapter 13 and read the parable of the sower. Close your eyes and open your imagination to farming of today. Here is what I see when I close my eyes. I see an average young man, about thirty years old, climbing off a John Deere tractor. The sun is blazing hot, and sweat is pouring from his body. He takes off his baseball cap then reaches into his back pocket and pulls out a handkerchief already drenched from his sweat, and wipes his forehead.

His face, neck, and arms are burned dark brown from long days in the sun. As he rests against the giant wheel of the tractor to catch his breath, he stares over his crops. He knows his days are numbered working in these fields for his dad because he feels the Heavenly Father calling him to different fields. He has felt this call for several years, but not until this day did he sense he was ready. Even in grade school in their small rural farming community he posed theological questions neither his teachers nor his pastor could answer. His parents were both proud and concerned. How would they send such a bright child to college on their meager savings? But then, toward the end of high school, he announced he didn't desire a college education.

Although startled by this announcement, his parents thought they would give him a few years to find himself. Perhaps when he was older he would attend college or join the military. But then several years turned into twelve. During this interlude of personal discovery, he didn't date, but instead worked tirelessly in devotion to the family farm.

Through his dedication, he took on more and more chores to allow his father a lighter work load. The man told him one day that every time he went to the barn or out to the pasture or walked to the corn fields, what he intended to do was already done. All that was left for him was to take his leave and relax, something he had to lean how to do, all because of his enterprising, benevolent son.

Returning to our young man again, we noticed something unique. He seemed to be preoccupied. Even when at rest, his mind wandered to a distant place. His father even commented on his distracted state as they strolled between the rows of corn where the young man would carefully brush the leaves away from his arms as though they were his children begging him to pick them up in his arms.

Planting seed had become so natural to him that he could accomplish the job with his eyes closed. He protected every seedling from the harsh weather elements as though each one was his delicate child. Day in and day out, he watched the corn sprout, grow, mature, and stand tall. His pride over the crop was like his parents watching him grow into maturity.

He gently caressed each row as a father caresses his children's cheeks or faces. Pausing at a clump of weeds, he'd yank the offenders out of the ground before they had a chance to harm his babies. He pruned and trimmed with the same devotion as a father would mentor one of his own children. Then he continued to walk, only lingering now and again to admire the field. Occasionally he'd stop to trim an unhealthy stem, or remove an isolated bug before it could feast on a virgin stalk. When he was satisfied with all he surveyed, he'd stroll along the rows, as pleased as any parent who cared for his children.

Suddenly a memory flashed into his mind. It was as goldenly vivid as the picturesque setting sun now before him on his farm. He recalled a beautiful garden dressed in a rainbow of colors, one full of all types of trees and plants and fruits and vegetables. After taking a deep breath, he recalled the freshness of the smell that only comes from a garden overflowing with healthy plants. There were animals of all types leisurely lounging, some sleeping. The irony was that these animals would today be predator and prey, but in this garden there was no enmity between them.

Among the perfection he spied a young man and woman just like him, perhaps a little older. They walked side by side holding hands, and appeared very happy. Laughing, teasing, and joking, they frolicked like Jack and Jill playing on a hill. But something was unique in their appearance next to him.

It was as though he were at two places at once. The couple was both beside him on his right side, and yet he could see himself walking with them simultaneously. At that precise moment he realized he was both God and man. His flesh was just as real as the young couple's, but his spirit recognized he was part of the Trinity, and he answered to the Father God.

A dream or reality?

About the time he asked himself this question, he emerged at the end of the row of corn. The answer solidified in his mind. Not a dream but his Father in heaven calling him to an awareness of who he really was and to his mission on earth.

Weighed down by sadness, the farmer in him returned to the present. Tomorrow, the fields would be harvested. He would miss the corn family he'd nurtured so long. Contrarily, he also felt happy knowing his crop was ready to leave his protective care and move on to a new life as food to feed hungry people all over the world.

Then, his mind moved forward thinking of how this field needed time to rest, lay fallow, until the next crop planting. Excitement filled his heart as he thought of the new family he would grow in the next season. But then his mind drifted to the spiritual realm as he lifted his head and gazed at the vast, endless starlit heavens.

He was neigh on thirty years of age, and he experienced a unique divine tug at his heart, a connection greater to his heavenly origin than his human life. He spent time late at night on a special hill where the sky appeared clearer, the stars were brighter, and the moon shone like a giant chandelier in the sky. And he prayed. He prayed so hard and long that perspiration saturated his clothing as though he were caught in a light rain shower. Perhaps he was in a shower, not of water but of purity. Not of dark clouds full of moisture, but heavenly white pillows filled with God's angels.

One night on his hill, he thought he heard his earthly father calling him like when he was a boy and he had to be summoned for supper. But then he realized it was not his daddy's voice but his Father in heaven who was calling him. The tug he'd felt on his heart turned out to be the Holy Spirit pulling him towards his original home in heaven. The more time he spent with his heavenly Father the more he realized the importance of his mission in life. He was born on the earth, not for tending crops in a field, but for rescuing souls in the darkness of an evil world.

Jesus was ready, prepared. Strong, hard, and lean. And he was single, thus free to devote his life to his Father's service. It was time to act.

If Jesus had been born into today's world, this is how I imagine him both as a man and as the Messiah. I don't think it matters that I didn't portray him as a carpenter. God could have chosen any blue-collar profession. What is important is that he was born common, simple, and plain, in a place where he learned discipline from working long, hard hours. This life prepared him for his mission on earth.

2

A Face of No Distinction

A simple face, a common face, one only so ordinary,
A face of no real distinction, yet how dare He!
Tanned by the sun, whipped by the wind, probably had acne.

So how could this face comment on the Torah at merely thirteen,
And make His elders take notice of a boy with a mind so keen?

It resisted temptation and confronted leaders of nations,
And did so without hesitation, to their great consternation.

It swiftly hushed boisterous crowds, bent on His demise,
And He walked through them unharmed as they beheld one so wise.

So who was this Man so mundane and commonly plain?
What gave Him the power and right to heal men's sin and shame?

The only answer is that He was the Messiah foretold,
And it was through His heavenly Father that He was so bold.

"But he walked right through the crowd and
went on his way." (Luke 4:30)

Jesus's dramatic exit described by Luke has to be the most powerful event in our Lord's ministry. You may wonder why I make
that statement when there are so many other exciting scenes

during his three-year sojourn. For instance, when Satan tempted Jesus. How about when he raised Lazarus from the dead, or his own resurrection from the tomb?

I agree there are countless sensational events in Christ's life, but let's examine the incident more closely.

Lights, camera, action. All is quiet on the set of a day in Jesus's life. Picture this. There is a mob—not a line of faithful admirers asking for his autograph. No, an aroused, angry, vengeful throng all wanting Jesus's hide to tan on the side of their adobe homes. Why where they angry? They were his BFFs as long as he preached what they wanted to hear. But then Jesus quoted scriptures to them. He read about Elijah who saved a widow from starvation, who was not a Jew, in Zarephath in the region of Sidon. Then he had the gall to heal Naaman the Syrian from leprosy, and again he was not a Jew. After these outrageous affronts, the crowd that once praised him in a synagogue in his home town of Nazareth suddenly turned on him. They were as hypocritical as a politician seeking election to an office. As long as Jesus tickled their ears with the lie that his countrymen were faithful God-fearing people, he was the greatest teacher they had heard in a long time. But when he began to preach about their sin of turning away from God, then he stepped on toes.

Now the masses wanted to murder Jesus. Hence, they took him out to the brow of the hill on which the town was built so they could push him off the cliff. And according to tradition, once he had fallen from the brow of the hill, they would stone him to death. And I don't mean they would toss a few pebbles. History records the Jews stoned violators of God's laws with brick-sized stones. Just to be sure their victims didn't survive, huge rocks were thrown on top of the bodies.

This was not just a lynch mob, but they were like a pack of wild dogs in Africa that smell the blood of their next meal, or like a Great White shark closing in on a wounded, bleeding seal not far from death. The multitude had already visualized a corpse at the bottom of the cliff. They were as vile as the Roman citizenry gathered in the coliseum to watch gladiators cut each other to ribbons.

But this mob was different.

Jesus's words had not only echoed in their ears but they had touched their souls. His words, although true, were even more difficult to swallow because Jesus was a home-town boy. Some of the mob probably had seen him as a boy playing in their village, with their own children now adults. As a boy growing up he may have spent the night at their homes on a sleep-over with one of their sons. At some point, he may have had a crush on one of their daughters. "He went to Nazareth, where he had been brought up, and on the Sabbath day he went into the synagogue, as was his custom. And he stood up to read." (Luke 4:16)

Why did he come home? According to Scripture, before his return to Nazareth of Galilee, he had just spent forty days in God's boot camp. Why do I call it a boot camp? Before the United States Marines allow their recruits to enter combat they have to undergo a rigorous training. Boot camp tests every recruit to the limits of his endurance. The training is designed to see if a recruit can survive the mental, emotional, and physical ordeal. Satan had tempted Jesus in every way possible. Jesus had not eaten a crumb during the forty days of temptation's boot camp. And the scriptures state he was hungry?

This fascinates me. The most I have gone without substantial food was for a two-week military training in the African bush. But even then, we still had something to eat from time to time. Once, I lost fifteen pounds in four days. To say I was hungry during this particular ordeal would have been an understatement. Looking at what Luke wrote about Jesus would also seem to be an understatement. Jesus being hungry was not the issue, only a minor point. In context, like anyone else, where do we head when we are exhausted? We go home. Exactly what Jesus did. He retired for a brief time so he could rest after his ordeal.

But then his own people become so angry they wanted to murder him. Look at what the Scripture says. "All spoke well of him and were amazed at the gracious words that came from his lips. 'Isn't this Joseph's son?' they asked." (Luke 4:22)

Think of his childhood. Here is a young man who grew up with their children and families. He ate in their homes, played with their children, sat with them in synagogue, and celebrated Jewish holidays. I bet some of the mothers nursed Jesus's wounds and dried his eyes when he cried as a boy. Then Jesus had the audacity to say after reading Isaiah 61:1–2 that he had fulfilled the prophecy recorded in the Scripture.

Blasphemy! How dare he say he was God's fulfillment of the Messiah.

You could hear the tone of their voices shifting from first gear of admiration to second gear of rage. Their third gear was filled with religious zeal, accelerating from zero to sixty while shifting into the fourth gear of rioting. Rubber burned on the back tires of their fury as they spun and smoked. Their bodies swayed from side to side like a racecar trying to gain traction before it lurches forward. Then once the angry crowd caught traction, they advanced on Jesus like a leopard on its unsuspecting prey.

You could see a once compassionate, supporting audience grotesquely evolve into an irrational mob. Previously caring arms that extended to embrace and love were now flailing with murderous ambition.

I am surprised that someone didn't pull a stiletto knife and stab Jesus in the heart before they reached the cliff where they intending to eliminate him.

Then, in the nick of time, at that moment between life and death, Jesus fearlessly faced down the crowd. His boldness wasn't rooted in revengeful strength or godly might to demonstrate he was their God. No, his strength was in an endless empathy for their misguided, bitter souls and an unconditional love for their derelict hearts. You might say his unshaken stance and unexplained exit was a foreshadowing of how he would forgive those who murdered him when they nailed him to the cross. Both angry crowds had no idea what they were doing, nor the eternal implications of their actions.

Dust billowed and swirled high into the air as the crowd rampaged like a herd of cattle in a blind stampede. The mob didn't engage in any theological contemplation or honest debate of truth. They were mindless and thoughtless, blinded by centuries of tradition that they felt must be upheld. Cultural tradition prevented them from seeing the Messiah, either with their eyes or their hearts.

Some angry participants had picked up a rock or two for good measure in case the fall didn't kill Jesus. A hardy thrust of a sizable rock on the forehead would finish him off. Children wailed, babies cried, old men wildly waved walking canes in the air. There might have been a few people in the crowd who were on Jesus's side. They also cried while asking the crowd to wait and listen to reason. But his supporters were pushed aside or trampled underfoot. Madness ensued.

Not a mortal madness, but a satanic, viral infection, currently immune to Godly treatment. Satan licked his wounds because he had not been able to persuade Jesus to follow him during the forty days of temptation.

Now, through this crowd, Satan saw a new opportunity. Why not pull off his favorite trick with humanity? He decided to use religious piety to murder the Messiah. Satan envisioned dark periods ahead, such as the Crusades and the Inquisition, during which he could employ self-righteousness to justify murder in the name of God.

If his second attempt to murder Jesus by manipulation of this crowd was a bust, at least the event may gain him some followers. After all, if this current mob didn't succeed, he planned to murder God's son on the cross in just under three years. Satan already knew the weakest mortal flaws from his success with Adam and Eve in the Garden—the most efficient killing machines were human pride, vanity, and self-righteous indignation.

Here's where the story explodes off the pages of the Bible. As I mentioned earlier, Jesus faced his accusers and then walked right through the crowd as quickly as a hot knife would cut through a stick of cold butter.

Can't you feel the shift in emotional and spiritual momentum? What we are missing, however, is what the Bible doesn't record.

First, why did Jesus let this crowd push him to the edge of the cliff? Isn't Jesus the son of God? Couldn't he have stopped the crowd before it began its dastardly work? So why did Jesus let this mindless mob kick him around like he was a rusty tin can? What was his point in permitting this hooliganism?

Second, how was Jesus able to stem the tide? Angry mobs are like herds of wild beasts. Cattle, horses, or buffalo don't stop once riled. Like I said earlier, they are mindless. So what was Jesus able to do in only a split second that paralyzed the crowd in mid-step and parted them like the Red Sea?

Third, what or who covered his back? The scriptures say not only did he walk right through them but he went on his way. How could a crowd be so enraged one minute and then *not* follow after him? Doesn't it make sense that once he took a few steps forward that someone in the crowd would have chased after him? And, implicit in this action, surely one person in the crowd would have followed after him and resumed his murderous madness?

I believe the answer to these three questions is found in Jesus's plain, ordinary face which was probably tanned, commonplace, and scared from accidents while playing when a young boy. Jesus's face was lean, strong, and resolute. It had to be, because he was determined not to be thrown off the precipice.

But I believe there is a more powerful answer. Just imagine the scene. In the time it takes to blink an eye, or thrust a knife, or push a man off a cliff, the mob saw God's face. How did they know it was God's face since none of them had seen God face to face? "You cannot see my face, for no one may see me and live." (Exodus 33:20)

Let me explain why I believe they knew it was God's face. What if one of them was transported two thousand years into the future and shown a car? How would he respond?

An object we give no second thoughts to suddenly becomes majestic and godlike to our visitor. This contraption must have come from another sphere because it can't be explained in his world. Yet this mixture of metal, plastic, and rubber is there on four wheels in front of him. Even though it's within arm's reach and he can see, feel, hear, and touch it, there are no words in his vocabulary to describe it. In the same manner, the mob realized there was something in Christ's face that was beyond their vocabulary of explanation and mortal experience.

In God's face, through Jesus, they glimpsed a brief portal into heaven. Like Moses in a sense, they didn't see God's face but only his back. (Exodus 33:20–23) In fact, the reason for this exciting wild-west showdown on the cliff was for one purpose. Jesus permitted it to happen so he could show them God. He had already informed them from the book of Isaiah while they had previously been in the synagogue *he* was God and they had rejected him. So now Jesus demonstrated he was God by subduing the mob and walking through them. A feat no mere mortal could achieve alone.

The crowd that day could have embraced the love of God and avoided their attempted murder of Jesus. But by choosing not to believe he was the Messiah, they fell into Satan's trap. Jesus then herded these self-righteous zealots like cattle into Satan's slaughter corral to accomplish his ends. They had to be shown God's power. When they saw the majesty of the Almighty, they were awestruck or perhaps dumbstruck.

But what caused the holy hypnotic trance the mob experienced by looking at his face? I have three ideas.

First, they encountered the enormity of God.

In Genesis 1:1 we read, "In the beginning God created the heavens and the earth." What really keeps me awake some nights are these questions. What was God's existence like before there was a heaven and earth? We know there was the Father, Son, and Holy Spirit, and possibly angels, but what was beyond infinity as we know it? Do man and God define infinity in the same way? What was before time as we know it? Since God exists outside of time, how does he define time? What are his thoughts about time? Why allow man to create a concept of time? The answer to these questions is outside our realm of thought.

> "For my thoughts are not your thoughts, neither are your ways my ways,' declares the Lord. 'As the heavens are higher than the earth, so are my ways higher than

your ways and my thoughts than your thoughts.'" (Isaiah 55:8–9)

Let me explain my point in another way. Before there was a universe, before what we know as void, before there was nothing as we define nothing, what was the Godhead's world like? Would the word *world* be a correct term to define where they lived? Was there a *where*? If so, could the *where* expand, contract, or invert? How did the Triune-God live, or can we even ask that question? If not, what is the definition of their *how*?

Jeremiah explained that God cannot be measured, confined, nor limited. "'Am I only a God nearby,' declares the Lord, 'and not a God far away? Can anyone hide in secret places so that I cannot see him?' declares the Lord. 'Do not I fill heaven and earth?' declares the Lord." (Jeremiah 23:23–24)

We know God is spirit, but what is spirit? Does spirit have matter or material? I think we cannot understand the substance of God's spirit because God lives outside our realm of existence that he created. Here's another question to pose concerning matter. Is it possible to know the meaning of matter as God knows it? Do man's and God's meaning of matter have the same definition?

What about the concepts of time and space? How do we know our definition agrees with God's understanding of these dimensions?

Let us again read in the book of Jeremiah and learn there are questions beyond our understanding. "'This is what the Lord says, he who made the earth, the Lord who formed it and established it—the Lord is his name. Call to me and I will answer you and tell you great and unsearchable things you do not know.'" (Jeremiah 33:2–3)

We need to ask ourselves as Christians, "What are these unsearchable things we do not know?" We can gain insight into this question by reading II Corinthians 12:1–4 where the Apostle Paul wrote, "I must go on boasting. Although there is nothing to be gained, I will go on to visions and revelations from the Lord. I know a man in Christ who fourteen years ago was caught up to the third heaven. Whether it was in the body or out of the body I do not know—God knows. And I know that this man—whether in the body or apart from the body I do not know, but God knows—was caught up to Paradise. He heard inexpressible things, things that man is not permitted to tell."

The realm beyond human understanding is further described in Ephesians 6:12 where the Apostle Paul pens, "For our struggle is not against flesh and blood, but against the rulers, against the authorities, against the powers of this dark world and against the spiritual forces of evil in the heavenly realms."

Another aspect of these unknown places is revealed in Lazarus's first resurrection from the dead. The events are recorded in John 11, and in verses 17 and 39 we discover that Lazarus was dead, and had been buried for four days. In fact, Martha, Lazarus's sister, didn't want to open the tomb at Jesus's command because she knew her brother's body would have started to decompose and would smell. Jesus told the men in the crowd to open the tomb anyway. Jesus commanded Lazarus to exit the tomb and he obeyed and was rejoined with his family.

Here to me is a very important question that I suppose could be addressed in doctoral dissertations. Where did Lazarus's soul spend the four days while his body was dead? I would also want to know, what did Lazarus do during his sojourn, with whom did he talk, and what did he learn? There are a host of other questions I could ask but will stop here.

There is one last story I want to discuss which is about the rich man and another man named Lazarus as recorded in Luke 16:19–31. In summary, the story relates that the rich man dies, and as a result of his selfish lifestyle, goes to hell, but Lazarus, although poor, goes to heaven because he lived a righteous life. The rich man asks Father Abraham to let Lazarus come down to hell and touch his tongue with water to quench his tortured soul. Abraham replies that his request is futile because both he and Lazarus made their choices in life.

Then Luke writes in verse 26, "And besides all this, between us and you a great chasm has seen fixed, so that those who want to go from here to you cannot, nor can anyone cross over from there to us."

Returning to Jeremiah's statement echoing what God told him to say, we find there are other realities that exist beyond what mortals experience on earth. We also learn that in these other realms there has been an eternal war between the forces of Satan and God over human souls. We can infer the battle began in the Garden and will continue until Christ's return. However, the most important lesson to be learned from the rich man and Lazarus is we have a choice while living to either follow God or Satan and we will be eternally rewarded accordingly.

Let me pose one last thought here about these realms beyond what we humans can understand. Could there be more than two? By this question I mean we know there is heaven and hell after physical life. However, could there be realms that we are not informed of beyond heaven, hell, and earth? If so, how many exist and what or who exists in them? Could these be the unsearchable things we do not know? If they are, just think what heaven will be like when God introduces these realms. I can hear God saying, "If you think heaven is grand, you haven't seen anything yet!"

Contemporary man is not the first to ask these questions. Listen to the wisdom of Solomon. "As you do not know the path of the wind, or how the body is formed in a mother's womb, so you cannot understand the work of God, the Maker of all things." (Ecclesiastes 11:5)

These questions may seem on the surface to be philosophical but I am not seeking to venture into the realms of St. Thomas Aquinas or other Christian philosophers. I only want to know what stopped that mob on the edge of that hill. I believe it was because they saw deity in Christ's face.

Second, they saw God in Christ's face.

Let me give you a true story to illustrate what I mean by the mob seeing God. Late one Friday night when we still lived in Rhodesia, a man called me, crying over the phone so much I could barely understand him. His sobbing seemed more from fear than sadness. I knew Henry from our mutual training for the Rhodesian

Army in Bulawayo. During my family's stay in the county, I had volunteered to serve as a medic. I offered to meet Henry at my home or a venue of his choosing, but he turned them down. He begged to meet me at our church building because it was the only place he felt safe. He was adamant and believed he would not be safe anywhere else except in the sanctuary of the church building.

Henry and I had spent three months in basic training and had learned to accept each other, regardless of our differences. We became privy to personal details about our marriages, families, jobs, and religious beliefs. Henry did not believe in God. He was not an atheist nor antagonistic toward Christians, and looking back now, he was probably an agnostic. So this is why it was very peculiar for him to demand to meet in the church building and nowhere else.

I arrived early and waited in the front of the auditorium. His wife entered first and then I saw she was helping him to walk as though he was paralyzed. Henry was bent over, hobbling like his legs were bound. He also bellowed all the way from the entrance until he stopped in front of the pulpit where I stood.

At first, I urged him to stop crying and attempted to help him straighten up. I was trying to treat him like a man who had just proudly finished basic army training. However, whatever he had experienced prior to his call to my house had literally crippled him.

Several minutes passed as Henry regained his composure. In his efforts to speak he was like a child who had scraped his knee. He wanted mommy and daddy, and his wife and me to make it all better. He literally could not vocalize a coherent word for at least fifteen minutes.

When he did begin to make some sense he related a story.

Henry and his wife, along with several other couples, were in a local bar celebrating the conclusion of basic training. They were having a great time, drinking, eating, and sharing stories. Then, a very attractive brunette woman, probably thirty-five or so, joined the party. It seems she was single and intriguing. I won't go into the details here but she was the self-appointed leader of a local quasi-religious Christian cult. She and her followers claimed no affiliation with conventional Protestant or Catholic groups.

Henry said as soon as he reached out and clasped her hand in greeting he felt an evil force travel up his arm. He couldn't move while he held her hand and all he could think of was getting away from her presence. Although he tried to free himself, he was frozen and fearful of not only losing his life, but his soul. He felt and believed her evil, posing as innocence, was dark, satanic, and spiritually deadly. Like a child, Henry felt helpless. He began crying, then weeping, and finally sobbing like a condemned man standing at the gallows.

He was so out of control from the time he met her that when he tried to call me, he had to have his wife assist him.

I had not met her before this night but we worked together to try and console Henry. In like manner, we both tried to reassure him which took over an hour. He was convinced he was a dead man because of the look he received from the cult leader. He believed her evil, masquerading as goodness, parasitically inhabited him and he wanted me to exorcise the evil out of him.

Henry only felt safe in the church because he believed the building was holy ground. He further believed the woman's evil could not work its power or defeat a *holy* man, which is how he viewed me, a pastor. His wife and I were finally able to convince him to move from the fetal position he assumed in the aisle to sitting in a pew. We then calmed him down as together we straightened him upright. Once he was in control of his faculties again, he and I talked. I was able to finally convince him that this woman had no power over him, nor could she take control of his soul.

I am convinced Henry saw Satan in this woman's face. Bulawayo was a small town of approximately a quarter million in 1976. I knew of this charlatan and, in fact, had met her once. Many local business men and women were part of her quasi-Christian following. After my hour-long meeting with her, I departed thinking about what Paul wrote in II Corinthians 11:14. "And no wonder, for Satan himself masquerades as an angel of light." I, too, felt as though I had been in the presence of an evil power.

I cannot explain my reaction. However, her impression on me at the time was one of a smart, manipulating charlatan. She was beautiful, educated, well-spoken, but seemed as slippery as an ocean eel. No matter how I tried to pinpoint different basic topics of faith, her replies were like a bar of soap in the shower that slipped all over the place.

She was as polished as a politician in what she said, but her answers were as empty as a flour sieve. Her words in conversation projected a communique of power and importance, but in the end were actually doublespeak.

Let's return to our story of Christ on the hill. The mob parted like the Jordon River when Israel crossed it to conquer Canaan. They moved aside, albeit unaware of their reason—they saw God in Christ's face. At first the mob was collectively emboldened through Satan's power. Satan had drawn the line in the sand, confronting God, but his followers succumbed to God's might.

There are two levels to consider in this story. At face value, the angry mob confronted Jesus and wanted to kill him. Jesus walked through their midst unharmed. The deeper story reveals one more battle in the continuing conflict between God and Satan, good and evil. Let's re-read Luke 4:30. "But he (Jesus) walked right through the crowd and went on his way." Jesus's departure, like piercing the enemy crowd with a spear, is an important truth for Christians. Whenever there's conflict between God and Satan, God always walks right through and goes on his way unharmed.

I would like to sum up the message of this story by referring to a conversation Jesus had with the Apostle Thomas.

> "Thomas said to him, 'Lord, we don't know where you are going, so how can we know the way?' Jesus answered, 'I am the way and the truth and the life. No one comes to the Father except through me. If you really knew me, you would know my Father as well. From now on, you do know him and have seen him.' Philip said, 'Lord, show us the Father and that will be enough for us.' Jesus answered: 'Don't you know me, Philip, even after I have been among you such a long time? Anyone who has seen me has seen the Father. How can you say, 'Show us the Father?' Don't you believe that I am in the Father, and that the Father is in me? The words I say to you are not

31

just my own. Rather, it is the Father, living in me, who is doing his work. Believe me when I say that I am in the Father and the Father is in me; or at least believe on the evidence of the miracles themselves.'" (John 14:5–11)

Third, they saw Christ before he had a human form and face. I'm suggesting that during the standoff, the mob was given a rare, one-time-only opportunity. Just as they were going to throw Jesus off the cliff, they were given a glimpse through a small window into heaven and saw the Savior as he was before he came to earth.

> "He who forms the mountains, creates the wind, and reveals his thoughts to man, he who turns dawn to darkness, and treads the high places of the earth—the Lord God Almighty is his name." (Amos 4:13)

How could they push the Being who created the cliff over it's edge? It was an impossible task, and they realized it. They were standing before the life-force that not only created the cliff, but their lives, and the planet upon which they lived.

I want us to pause here for a moment and consider what a sacrifice Jesus made to wear a human face. What are the words that come to mind that describe when the infinite puts on the face of the finite? There are none. How does the perfect fit into the imperfect? It's impossible. The closest analogy I can think of is of a man who wears a size thirteen shoe who attempts to try on a baby's shoe. However, in Christ's case, the baby shoe fit just fine. Now try to imagine that perfect being who knows no constraints donning the worse constraint possible—a human being with flesh and bone.

Voluntarily, Jesus gave up being deity in order to become human, which is beyond anything we can comprehend. In fact, the greatest minds of all time can't grasp the pure energy of who lives behind the face the mob beheld on that cliff. That face, which had known no human form until he consented to live on earth, knew the names of every person trying to murder him. That face knew details of their lives before they were born, knew the number of hairs on each body, and how their lives served in his father's universal plan. That face not only knew their lives up to and beyond their deaths, he knew their ancestors and descendants.

The face the mob beheld could have spoken one word or blinked an eye and the crowd would have disappeared or dropped dead. That face could have eliminated the town of Nazareth, wiping it off the face of the earth like Sodom and Gomorrah. The same power he had to raise the dead, restore sight to the blind, and calm the tempestuous seas could have squashed the mob like a bug under an elephant's foot. Yet, that face chose to spare the multitude and merely walk through them like they weren't there.

Our Savior's face would later be beaten, would feel blood slowly dripping down his forehead and into his eyes from the crown of thorns. The face that whispered, "It is finished," during his last moments on earth, could have done oh, so much more to the crowd, but chose not to. Why did he bestow grace on the mob and not punishment? There can only be one answer—that face will be *the* face each member of the mob will kneel before on the final day.

To have all this power and might yet demonstrate constraint, to literally control the sun, moon, and stars—because he created them. To have life, not just as we know it, but to be the one who breathed life into clay. To walk in mortal temptation but never sin in word, thought, or deed. To stand before kings knowing they will all bow before him one day. These facts don't begin to explain the power of Christ before he had a face.

And because of this power there are still marvelous things yet to be revealed that were planned long ago. "O Lord, you are my God; I will exalt you and praise your name, for in perfect faithfulness you have done marvelous things, things planned long ago." (Isaiah 25:1)

3

Eyes with Vision Beyond Sight

Behold the eyes of our Savior!
Two orbs of mortal flesh, first opened in a manger.

Before they were commonly human, what sights had they known?
Heaven's creation is where they had grown.

Then they were subjected to earth's wind, rain, and fire,
They were like all men's eyes, tempted with earthly desire.

Probably blinded or irritated at least once or twice
By sawdust blown in them by being too close to a carpenter's vise.

At thirty, they searched deep into hearts, motives, and thoughts,
Nothing could escape their understanding of how man avoids his oughts.

The trial, the beating, the trail of tears as He was laden with the cross,
All through this torment no anger but pity He felt for mankind's
spiritual loss.

Then, from on high nailed to a tree upon that cursed hill Golgotha,
He saw beyond eternity all who loved Him, including a woman
named Martha.

Then, his last breath expelled as He closed His eyes as a
human one last time,
But they were opened three days later, never to close again
as our Master divine.

"However, as it is written: 'No eye has seen, no ear has heard, no mind has conceived what God has prepared for those who love him.'" (1 Corinthians 2:9; Isaiah 64:4)

When I was a child in the late 1950s and 60s I would spend every last penny I had on plastic model airplanes. I loved the models with hundreds of parts that I pried off the plastic tree and then glued together. Each part was clearly labeled with a number which was located in a set of instructions. If you followed the instructions, each piece could be glued together with minimal effort.

However, I never read the instructions. I preferred the challenge of figuring out by examining the pictures of the airplane on the box where the parts fit to make the whole model. I didn't like reading, and to this day if I purchase something with instructions I rarely read them. My wife still asks, "Did you read the instructions?" To which I answer under my breath, "No dear, I can put it together."

Personal reflection led me to realize I had nothing against instructions per se, and yet, through trial and error, I eventually put the pieces of my plane together. Once completed, I painted it, affixed the decals, and hung it from the ceiling in my room. But why did I refuse the instructions? I enjoyed the challenge of mentally picturing how the pieces fit into the finished product. You might say these models were not assembled by sight as in following the instruction, but by intuition, touch, and judgment. Sight was necessary but only part of the five senses required to enjoy what my whole one dollar purchased.

I am told that mechanics working on large engines rely on touch when they can't see where to restore parts to their proper place. Surgeons learn to feel inside the human body cavity where internal organs should be. Experienced doctors can prod the outside of a person's body and make decisions about the disposition of an organ without seeing it. It's thought musicians who practice intensely on their instruments develop neural pathways from their fingers to their brains. These pathways contribute to producing music, and sight is not involved. There are blind musicians and vocalists who cannot *see* the music but can hear the notes inside their heads. Makes one wonder if eyes are necessary although we live in a sighted world. These exceptional adaptations give new meaning to what the Apostle Paul wrote in II Corinthians 5:7 "We live by faith, not by sight."

We are told no eyes have seen what God has prepared for those who love him. I believe he won't allow us to see his heavenly preparation because our human eyes wouldn't understand what they were viewing. Of course, by leaving it a mystery, we accept our home by faith and not by sight.

Let me explain. On my first trip home to the USA after spending two years in Rhodesia, friends and family would ask one question. "What was it like?" When I enthusiastically related alien customs, culture, climate, and experiences from Africa, I noticed a zombie-gaze embrace my listeners. Their eyes glazed over and they stared off into space as though in a hypnotic trance.

Their facial expressions communicated they either didn't believe a word I said, or they could not grasp the concepts I shared. Finally, I stopped sharing my experiences and would change the subject if I were asked. To this day, as I write this chapter, there are many incidents I have never shared with anyone.

I long pondered this phenomenon. Then the answer dawned on me one day. The people who asked me these curiosities had no frame of reference. They had rarely traveled outside of America, much less out of Texas. Others folks may have been overseas, but only traveled in Europe. Furthermore, they traveled overseas as visitors on vacation. So their only experience of local culture was through American tourist glasses. They were isolated from the common population of the poorer or middle class because they experienced only hotels and tour groups.

I, on the other hand, had lived, worked, and toiled with the local populace. I knew how much a loaf of bread cost, where to purchase shoes, how to pay a monthly mortgage, and most importantly, what was considered polite and impolite cultural etiquette. I realized several consequences of my African sojourn.

First, I had become bi-cultural which meant I was able to speak and think in two cultures at the same time. A bi-cultural person will know the expected etiquette of two different cultures simultaneously, then he or she will speak and act accordingly following the rules of each in judicious application.

Second, I no longer viewed life and history solely from an American perspective. Christmas, Easter, Thanksgiving, and July Fourth are special holidays for most Americans. However, although Christmas and Easter are universal in the global Christian calendar, different cultures have different ways of celebrating those holidays. Thanksgiving and July Fourth are uniquely American and have no special meaning outside of United States soil. For example, how many Americans celebrate Bastille Day or know why Guy Fawkes day is important in the British culture?

What is true about holidays is also true about world events. I will never forget a time when I overheard some Rhodesian friends lambasting our American president. I asked why they were being so hard on him, and they explained his decisions and policies from their view as Rhodesians. When I listened to their reasoning, I, too, became angry at him although I was an American.

Third, something interesting occurs to an American's psyche when living within a non-American population as the minority. His world view as an American begins to change when he follows the principles Paul wrote about in I Corinthians 9:19–23. "Though I am free and belong to no man, I make myself a slave to everyone, to win as many as possible. To the Jews I became like a Jew, to win the Jews. To those under the law I became like one under the law (though I myself am not under the law), so as to win those under the law. To those not having the law I became like one not having the law (though I am not free from God's law but am under Christ's law), so as to win those not having the law. To the weak I became weak, to win the weak. I have become all things to all men so that by all possible means I might save some. I do all this for the sake of the gospel, that I may share in its blessings."

Fourth, my personal frame of reference about my own American culture was permanently restructured. The people with whom

I spoke in the USA couldn't comprehend these cultural encounters I had experienced. What I realized was that once anyone has lived in and not just visited another culture, that experience alters his or her perception. Like film in a camera, once an image is exposed to the light it cannot be changed. It is permanently burned into the film. When talking to my friends and family I was not aware of how these experiences had changed me, and therefore, did not take that fact into consideration.

Let's make a comparison with my original cultural grounding and the home God has prepared for us. If we try to grasp what our home in heaven will be like while still in this life, we would have no frame of reference. Even if God tried to explain in our native language we would not be able to understand. Hence, we accept our eternal home by faith and not by sight. Once in heaven, we will never want to exchange that abode for any other place God created.

This sightless preparation is what Paul wrote about in 1 Corinthians 2:7 "No, we speak of God's secret wisdom, a wisdom that has been hidden and that God destined for our glory before time began." He then later writes in verses 10–11, "but God has revealed it to us by his Spirit. The Spirit searches all things, even the deep things of God. For who among men knows the thoughts of a man except the man's spirit within him? In the same way no one knows the thought of God except the Spirit of God."

I hope by now you are beginning to grasp what vision Jesus had as the Son of God living in the flesh. He had unlimited intuition, perception, grasp, and understanding. Every person he met, every situation he was in, he knew the outcome before it happened. In fact, he knew the outcome before creation, before time, before any possible conception of what we regard as creation or time. Do we dare attempt to broach the mind of God? It's not possible for the finite to understand the infinite. Solomon wrote, "As you do not know the path of the wind, or how the body is formed in a mother's womb, so you cannot understand the work of God, the maker of all things." (Ecclesiastes 11:5) Even with today's technology man cannot grasp even a smidgen of what God has set in motion through his creation.

But we still need to try to understand the works of God because in this attempt we draw closer and closer to insight of his world. "Open my eyes that I may see wonderful things in your law." (Psalm 119:18)

Let me offer you an earthly example. One day during my stint with the Rhodesian Army, we'd been on a walking patrol and by nightfall, we were all exhausted. Our corporal picked a spot to rest for the night next to a dry riverbed. We spread out along the bank, surrounded by brown, withered brush. Several chaps joined me on a rocky outcrop which formed a ledge where the water had washed away the soil thousands of years ago.

In the fading light, one of the men noticed paintings on the rock face that had probably been there for hundreds or maybe thousands of years. They were stick figures of men and animals obviously drawn to communicate a message. All I could do was sit there and stare in awe. Suddenly, I was no longer on patrol in 1978, but catapulted back through time to an age devoted to tribal hunting and gathering. Those paintings were not from a history book nor in a museum display, but right before me, pristine and raw. Only an anthropologist could interpret what they meant. I wasn't tired any longer but felt energized. The eyes of my spirit saw an entirely different scene around our camp.

I turned to face the dry riverbed and imagined abundant water flowing, and a tribal encampment around this precious resource. I could envision why the people chose this site for their village. From this location they could hunt and gather food, and lead a satisfyingly simple life. To some degree, I actually envied them.

At one time children played where we were sitting. Women gathered drinking water for their families in the cool of the morning. Men searched for flint for spear heads. The area in my imaginings was green and not brown. It was populated with people, cattle, and goats, with huts, and kraals for the animals, and not isolated and overgrown with brush and trees.

Questions that only God could answer ran through my mind. When did the people leave this area, and where did they go? What caused the river to run dry? During the time that this area was occupied and vibrant, could there have been feuds between rival tribes fighting over these resources?

The most important questions seemed to shout at me. What happened to the people who drew these paintings? What motivated them? What were they trying to communicate? Could these paintings have come from an inner need all humans have to say, "I'm here! I matter! I want to leave something behind so people will know I lived."

I'm reminded of the words of the Psalm writer. "'Show me, O Lord, my life's end and the number of my days; let me know how fleeting is my life. You have made my days a mere handbreadth; the span of my years is as nothing before you. Each man's life is but a breath.'" (Psalm 39:4–5)

Could my African bush experience be close to offering a partial understanding of how God views our world from his abode? I would never have had a glimpse into the past of a world not my own had I not examined that rock painting. "But do not forget this one thing, dear friends: With the Lord a day is like a thousand years, and a thousand years are like a day." (II Peter 3:8)

Finally, it also causes me to reflect that *sightedness* is highly overrated. Yes, eyesight allows us to pursue the daily mundane chores, but in many ways, it serves as a blinder to prevent us from seeing the eternal. Perhaps this is why the Apostle Paul wrote in II Corinthians 4:18, "So we fix our eyes not on what is seen, but what is unseen. For what is seen is temporary, but what is unseen is eternal."

If we are to understand God, then we need to first see how he sees. Furthermore, see *what* he sees, view consequences as he made them. We need to divest ourselves of this mortal shell we call human flesh and bone and attempt to become pure spirit as he is spirit. Only then will we be able to assimilate his call to justice, mercy, and judgment. But not as perfect as he is, but as imperfect seeking to be perfect. "He has showed you, O man, what is good.

And what does the Lord require of you? To act justly and to love mercy and to walk humbly with your God." (Micah 6:8)

How can we put on the *skin of God* to understand his spiritual sight? He is spirit and we are physical. Try as we might, we cannot grasp spirit and soul when we know only the physical. Like children, his children, we have spiritual sight modeled for us through his word. But even in our most astute attempt, we are still only guessing. Our finite exploration of God's sight is like a flea firmly imbedded between an elephant's toes surrounded by darkness. His sight leads him to believe his world is safe and secure until the elephant steps into water.

Then the flea suffers a rude awakening. He needs to adjust his sight in his world to the potential of a world beyond what he knows. Therefore, we, like this flea, need to emerge from our darkness to see what is beyond the toes of our ignorance, what we once thought were safe and secure.

Although it's not possible to have God's vision, it's the effort of viewing the world from his perspective that draws us closer to him. The flea may pull himself out of darkness so that he is aware of the size of the elephant's foot, but there's still so much more to the elephant that he can't and will never be able to see. So how do we pierce our blindness to improve our sight into what God sees? Here's my suggestion.

Once in 1976 while visiting wounded soldiers in a hospital ward in Bulawayo, I came across a young man with a tragic story. Stan and his friend were riding in their Land Rover through the bush in a rural part of Rhodesia and hit a land mine. The young man lost his sight, but his long-time friend was killed instantly by the blast. Stan also sustained shrapnel wounds, which would soon heal, while the hope for sight was dashed by permanent injury.

As a child, Stan had lived in the bush country of Rhodesia and spent much of his time with the Ndebele tribe, a branch of the Zulu tribe, with a similar language. He reached manhood speaking both English and Sindebele fluently. Stan loved the outdoors and he took a job working for the Rhodesian government as a game park manager. During his hospital stay, I spent two days with him and his wife, trying to help them over the shock of learning about his permanent blindness. Sometime later, I learned that his marriage ended in divorce—collateral damage from his injury. Stan moved to the Republic of South Africa and took a job as a court translator.

Although this is a heartbreaking story, I think it offers insight into *seeing as God sees*. Here is a blind man who sees without his eyes. And without his eyes, he sees much deeper into the Ndebele culture than most sighted people. His sight is not only in the language of the Zulu, but into their minds where physical eyes are of no value. Stan's life experience allowed him to serve as a translator of the language, but also of their values, morals, beliefs, customs, and etiquette. His story demonstrates how we can begin to see the remainder of the elephant.

I believe we can understand how God sees a little better by reading two passages from Psalms.

> How can a young man keep his way pure? By living according to your word. I seek you with all my heart; do not let me stray from your commands. I have hidden your word in my heart that I might not sin against you. (Psalm 119:9–11)

> Open my eyes that I may see wonderful things in your law. I am a stranger on earth; do not hide your commands from me. My soul is consumed with longing for you laws at all times. (Psalm 119:18–20)

4

Ears Not Only for Heavenly Sounds

Try to imagine sound before there was time and Heaven.
Was it as perfect as Hebrews believed of the number seven?

Would it have been possible to be heard by the human ear?
Or, are their perceptions beyond what we can hear?

Who spoke to God before He created His winged innocents?
Could there have been others before them with other types of senses?

Now think of the audible sacrifice Jesus made by becoming human,
Because He left his perfect union of three to be a Jew among the pagan.

He was willing to taste earthly life, what it meant to live in human form,
Which He began in a smelly manger, ushered from the womb, a newborn.

He made this audible offering for you and me,
Because He listened to His Father's command to sacrifice self
for our eternity.

––––––––––––––

"And I know that this man—whether in the body or
apart from the body I do not know, but God knows—
was caught up to paradise. He heard inexpressible
things, things that a man is not permitted to tell."
(II Corinthians 12:3,4)

Not too long ago, a young couple come to my office for marriage counseling. One of their issues was their five-year-old son. Seems he was an angel at school and all his teachers loved him, but at home he was defiant and didn't respect personal boundaries. They also reported he thrived in quiet situations, but that loud noises made him cover his ears, and at times, if the commotion continued, he would scream as if in pain. I suggested that he may be exhibiting signs of Autism, and that they should take him to a doctor for examination.

In counseling sessions, Christian therapists are often asked how do people know whether or not the voices they hear are coming from God. Frankly, I don't know. One of the characteristics of people diagnosed with schizophrenia is hearing voices. They often exhibit a stated or implied fascination with the heavenly realm focusing on God or Satan.

Although some people diagnosed with schizophrenia claim to hear God's voice, there are many people who don't have this diagnosis who claim the same thing.

The most often described ways of hearing God is through meditation, prayer, listening to your own heart, or the reading of God's Word. There are many books on the subject, ranging from scholarly works to practical self-help books. Then there are people who believe they hear God in their dreams or in their visions. Some people will talk to God out loud in front of anyone without reservation or embarrassment. Others will state frankly and boldly that God gave him or her some message on some topic or issue and claim direct communication. Usually, it's a communication that only the recipient can hear. I have no desire to question or dispute these beliefs as frankly I'm neither a scholar nor an expert in this field.

Whether humans can hear actual words coming from the mouth of God or not, have you ever wondered what other sounds might swirl in the heavenly realms? I'm not referring to singing, praising, worshiping, or any other ways of exalting God. All of these forms of worship we are told by scripture currently happen and will continue after the resurrection. The question that baffles me is what other sounds in heaven did Jesus willingly give up to come to earth?

I know that conversations occur between God and the subjects of his realm, and with Satan, as these are recorded in Scripture. Job, for example, was a target of calamity as a result of a conversation between God and Satan. We also know God spoke to Moses and other religious leaders, such as David, Abraham, and prophets such as Isaiah and Jeremiah. But what I want to know is could there be sounds and languages unique to heaven, different from any human communication on earth? By this question I don't necessarily mean a difference in dialect or language, but a whole other way of communicating.

When I ponder heaven's language, I try to reach beyond my limitations of mortality. Common sense says language, thoughts, culture, emotions, feelings, ideas, and perceptions have to be of a unique distinction in heaven. At the very least, not only different, but perfect because God is perfect. This fact in and of itself infers difference. For example, what is heard in heaven may not necessarily be confined to the spoken word. And to use the phrase *spoken word* may have an entirely different application in a perfect kingdom such as God's.

Let me explain. When we lived in Rhodesia, not only were there a variety of tribal languages, but each one had a unique musical flow. Years later during my deployment to Afghanistan, there were also many different dialects, and again, each with its own distinct musicality.

I've concluded there is an exclusive fluidity in every society, a type of culturally specific rhythm, mood, disposition, and body language which are all connected to language. Although I am only fluent in English, when I was around people who spoke a different language, I was fascinated and in awe. I can remember sitting in a mud hut in Rhodesia, closing my eyes, and being serenaded by the sounds of the MaShona words.

When a cultural outsider spoke in a local tongue he not only knew the language, he seemed to transform his mind into the thought patterns of the tribe with whom he spoke. Language is more than grammar. It is a style of thinking that adds two plus two to equal four in their own culturally specific way. This simple mathematic equation will always have the same sum, but how each culture arrives at this sum may be different.

For example, when I observed a traditional MaShona funeral mixed with bits and pieces of Christian customs, mourning and grieving were expressed in measures my western thinking would call histrionic.

Another time, I witnessed an ancestral worship ceremony in a rural village. It consisted of their culturally assumed spiritual possession of a local tribesman with his fellows supervising his transformation. From my previous research on this topic I learned they believed an ancestral spirit possessed the man. After several minutes the ritual participants moved on to another area to have solitude. My MaShona African guide informed me I was not permitted to follow the group of worshipers because I was an outsider and a white man.

Was this African man in a self-induced psychotic state? Were the men surrounding him in a shared psychotic disorder? Could there really be a world of demons, or at the very least evil spirits, that they allowed into their souls? As a Christian, I believe in another dimension where God and Satan battle for every human's soul. Strictly speaking, as a therapist, I would diagnose shared psychotic disorder. But who am I to judge? Don't Christians believe in the indwelling of God's Holy Spirit? Don't we believe his Spirit guides us and rules our lives as we grow spiritually? So do the people of this tribe. The difference being that the MaShona believe their ancestors must be appeased and served in order to avoid punishment. Christians, on the other hand, have a loving God and Savior in Jesus Christ, and our worship comes from an appreciation for having our sins forgiven.

What voices or sounds did these traditional tribal men hear? Was it a single spirit or many spirits? In addition to the spirit or spirits, what other voices or sounds from their ancestor's world where part of their worship? Did their ancestors speak to them audibly or through their hearts devoted to what I would call a pagan practice? As a Christian, I would view their worship as Satanic in origin, but as a counselor, I would feel they were experiencing self-induced auto-hallucinations. Also as a Christian, I believe Christ would not want me to condemn, but to understand so that I could reach them with Jesus.

Heavenly Noise:

My next question may seem humorous, but I pose it in all sincerity. Since God is everywhere, where does he go to have some peace and quiet? Since he is omnipresent, where would his private place be located? After all, I imagine he must grow tired of our infantile behavior on earth. In fact, could we not say it would be impossible for him to have a quiet place? Or, because he is God, he could create a condition where he could have his quiet place simultaneously with being omnipresent because he is omnipotent!

We humans need some alone time, so how would God separate himself from everywhere to have his private time? I know he is perfect therefore he does not suffer from fatigue of any kind as we humans do, but we read in his relationship with Moses he does feel anger. The Scriptures record in Exodus chapter 32 that God became so angry with the tribe of Israel he wanted to wipe them from the face of the earth and start over with Moses. Why did he want to take this action? Because he was so fed up with Israel complaining and disobeying, but Moses talked him out of punishing them.

So if God feels this angry, he must feel other emotions as well. We read of his love, forgiveness, compassion, mercy, and many other emotions. And along with emotions of virtue there must also be states of exhaustion. We know God rested on the seventh day after creation. But I wonder, does God rest the same way his creation rests? If not, what does God in rest look like? If he is all powerful then why did he need rest? Was his rest symbolic to set an example, or did he really need to rest? Either way, there was and is constant effort or work on God's part dealing with us humans.

Anyone looking at our history has to conclude that there must have been many times when God wanted to scrap all of his creation and start over. So, like the child with autism who covers his ears because of loud noises, does God ever cover his ears? That is, if he indeed has ears to cover. Since he is spirit and not flesh, we would have to ask how he would block auditory sensation.

Loud and Quiet in Heaven:

Is all sound in heaven the same as sound on earth? If I answered this question, I would have to say, "No," but I have no proof. My limited reason as a Christian believer assumes there must be sounds in heaven that are exclusive to that domain, spiritual sounds that we will enjoy after the resurrection. I pose another question. Does God hear in the same manner we his creation hear? I'm not suggesting God has the same internal anatomical organs for hearing as we do because I don't believe he does. Regardless of how sound is heard and processed by God, does the resonance have the same meaning, interpretation, and impact on him as it does to us mortals?

Let me give you some examples. Are God's ears more sensitive to a baby's cry or a lion's roar? Which was louder to God's ears—Mt. St. Helen exploding, or prayers offered by the people who suffered from its eruption? How loud are the cries of babies dying in abortion clinics? To what sound could their cries be compared? Are the prayers of soldiers in the midst of battle louder than the combat itself?

When a needle or tiny sewing pin falls and hits the floor does it sound like continents colliding or mountains crumbling to God? What is the sound of a thread going through the eye of a needle? Have you heard this sound? I haven't but God has.

Do exploding atoms pop like firecrackers to God? Or, do they make any sound at all to the one who made them? He can also choose not to hear their noise whereas we can't. Speaking of atoms exploding, when molecules separate, what noise do they make in God's ear? Think of this. When plants bloom or when trees grow, how loud is the noise of their growth in God's ears, and what sounds would they make to human ears if we could hear them? Since God is not bound by time, does he hear as each ring is formed in every tree trunk?

For me personally, I can't wait until I am in heaven to hear all of these sounds and many others found only in God's realm, known to him from the beginning of time and creation.

Emotions and Sounds:

I read years ago that a fetus in its mother's womb is either negatively or positively impacted by its mother's emotions. If the mother is in an abusive relationship, the baby feels her fear, or if the mother is in a healthy relationship, the baby feels her joy, which to me means sounds are associated with emotions. What are these sounds? In our mortal world, sounds associated with abuse are crying, screaming, and yelling, all of which in context lead to shock, grief, depression, anxiety, and sometimes suicide.

God hears the sounds from a large masculine hand as it slaps a wife's face. This is followed by the sound of her falling to the floor, possibly hitting her head against furniture. What about the sound of a knee as it kicks the side of a wife falling to the floor, or the sound the angels hear as a large shoe kicks and breaks a woman's ribs?

All these sounds and more are heard by a heavenly host twenty-four hours a day, seven days a week. Yes, there is the sound of the actual brutal conflict, but could there be a second, separately unique sound beyond human ears? Could it be that pain from this abuse has a sound that only the holy can hear? Do these sounds hurt our heavenly Father's ears and cause angels to weep?

As emotions accompanied by their associated sounds are felt by a fetus, could it be that we humans have sounds associated with our emotions that only God can hear?

For example, when we are in a state of happiness, does God hear something different from us than when we are sad? When we are depressed, does our depression create a special, unique wave of sound different than when we are anxious? When we cry, does God hear the falling of our tears as they roll down our cheeks before they are whipped away? Do the sounds of tears of joy differ from the sounds of tears of sorrow in God's hearing? In short, what sounds do we give off in our emotions that are sensitive only to God's ears? Would these sounds of holy sensitivity be exclusive to the Triune or would other heavenly beings hear them as well?

Let's probe deeper. Does jealousy have one distinct sound to God that might be different from envy? How about hate and love? Do they create distinct and different sounds to God? What about rage, anger, lies, and deceit? Do these each sound differently to treachery? How about honesty, goodness, love, compassion, and holiness? Do they each have their own unique sound to God?

The point I'm making is that I believe that the language of heaven entails more than the spoken languages on earth. I think heavenly language is full of color, density, and substance beyond human understanding. Language to those who populate heaven is not limited to the audible, so it does not require hearing as we hear. They hear through their senses and emotions in addition to how we understand hearing.

When Jesus was sent to earth, he sacrificed this richness as deity in hearing for you and me. I can't prove it, but when you think beyond the traditional sounds of heaven and earth, the holiness of hearing uniquely as God hears will belong to Christians on that final day.

Heavenly Language of Sensitivity:

"And now I will show you the most excellent way. If I speak in the tongues of men and of angels, but have not love, I am only a resounding gong or a clanging cymbal." (I Corinthians 13:1)

Over my years as a counselor, I have noticed one trait about doctors that has fascinated me. As they grow older, many develop hobbies in either art or music or both. Any medical student who is going to succeed has to have above average skills in mathematics because this discipline is so involved in chemistry, physics, and biology. Here is an observation I have about what happens to a doctor after years of practicing medicine. I believe he or she not only finds relaxation in these arts, but something more—personal fulfillment.

I think in their creative need they want to see more than healing in their patients. They crave the need to see a finished piece of art or music that they can own, and can say, "I made this. It's my creation."

Could it be that beyond the academics of medical school, the practical application of their therapeutic *art* is that they hear something in their souls? Could it be that the language of math, science, and art begins to connect and is heard within the human spirit? Could it be that the creation of art and music is the aesthetic energy that can only be expressed by what is heard in the heart, that only those connected in this unique vernacular can understand?

I don't believe this outgrowth of an artistic display of the soul and spirit is planned. I think it's an accumulation over decades where the magic of art, mathematics, and science come together in a jubilant sympathy. They then play and dance in harmonious concert. And this is all because of what these medical professionals hear in their hearts and souls.

I think this sensitivity of hearing a language not spoken by the human tongue, but felt by the heart, soul, and spirit is the closest analogy we have to the nature of the language heard in heaven. And it's not even the tip of the iceberg. In fact, it's not even an ice cube. As I wrote earlier, what mortal can understand what is heard exclusively in heaven? I believe when God, his angels, and Jesus were forced to use human language they found the experience as crude and primitive as if we tried to use a flint knife to cut our food, or had to rub two sticks together to start a fire.

One Sound, One Voice:

"My sheep listen to my voice; I know them, and they follow me." (John 10:27)

Several years ago, my wife and I were blessed to vacation in New Zealand and Australia. One of the ventures we booked was to spend three days and nights on a sheep station in the outback. Words cannot adequately describe the experience. I think the most interesting memory I have personally was when we rode with William, the station operator, all over his land.

As we approached a watering hole, he said, "I think a sheep's purpose in life to to see how quickly it can kill itself." He elaborated that sheep are the dumbest animals he had ever seen.

All of William's time was spent in keeping the sheep alive. He had to travel over hundreds of acres to various feeding areas to be sure they had food. We visited in winter, but even during the sparse rainy season, natural grasses weren't enough and without the extra food the sheep would starve. "The Lord is my shepherd, I shall lack nothing. He makes me lie down in green pastures." (Psalm 23:1,2a)

At first, I thought his statement was harsh, but after spending hours with him and observing what he had to do on a daily basis, I began to understand what he meant. There is a vast underground artesian basin under that part of Australia. Sheep station owners would drill wells in strategic places so that the sheep would never be too far from the vital resource they needed for survival. "He leads me besides quiet waters." (Psalm 23:2b)

Throughout the trip, we saw sheep that were stuck in the mud along creeks, or around watering holes. They would wander too far into the water and their fleece coats would become saturated, making them too heavy to move. Without the assistance of William and his men, the sheep would starve, and their rotting carcasses would pollute the water supply. Sheep don't watch where they are going and tend to follow one another even into danger. "He guides me in paths of righteousness for his name's sake. Even though I walk through the valley of the shadow of death, I will fear no evil, for you are with me; your rod and your staff, they comfort me." (Psalm 23:3b–4)

Toward the end of the day, we drove up to a huge reservoir. The 500 or so sheep surrounding the water scattered at our approach. We remained in the vehicle and were mesmerized at what happened next. Suddenly, a cacophony of bleating and baaing arose like I'd never herd before or since. William explained the ewes and lambs had been separated when they spread out. Now their bleating was so loud we could hardly hear ourselves think.

As time went on, the bleating took on a unique pattern. We'd hear a baa from one point, then an answering bleat from another section of the mob. Soon the individual calls grew closer and closer to each other. Eventually, each lamb found its mother as the pairs connected. It was one of the most amazing observations of nature. William explained that each lamb knew its mother's voice and could ferret it out among all the confusion of hundreds of sheep.

The Scriptures tell us, "For the Lord himself will come down from heaven, with a loud command, with the voice of the archangel and with the trumpet call of God, and the dead in Christ will rise first. After that, we who are still alive and are left will be caught up with them in the clouds to meet the Lord in the air. And so we will be with the Lord forever. Therefore encourage each other with these words." (I Thessalonians 4:16–18)

Somehow I believe we will know our Lord's voice like each lamb knew its mother's voice. It will also be the beginning of an introduction to hearing some of the most beautiful and wonderful sounds that have ever graced the human ear. These perfect, holy sounds from heaven have been reserved only for those who know their Shepherd's voice, and will only be audible after the resurrection.

5

Arms That Embrace the Universe

Oh, man, here's a thought somewhat strange,
The arms that hold you did the universe arrange.

Before they were appendages of flesh to grasp and hold,
What we know as the universe they did creatively mold.
No telling what else they did mortal flesh couldn't behold.

So think about the sacrifice our Savior made for His spiritual kin
When He left heaven to become human to save us from sin.

These same arms that knew the stars and galaxies above,
Raised the dead, healed the blind, yet gently held a turtle dove.

Then, they were stretched end to end on a cross of wood,
And nailed in a death Satan thought he had arranged and understood.

In three days their strength was restored as Jesus rose from the grave,
Defeating death and Satan at his own game, this terrible knave.

And now these powerful, gentle arms usher us to heaven above,
To be with God and Jesus where there is a final, eternal love.

My Daddy's arms were always a safe place. As a boy when I was scared, it was his arms in which I sought shelter. When I was hurt, it was his arms that enveloped me like a star fish. When imaginary monsters were after me, his arms shot out bolts of lighting and killed them all. I can recall one time when I was very sick and my parents brought me home from the doctor. I had a high fever and whimpered between bouts of sobbing. As I lay on the backset, my eyes partially closed, I recall being scooped up like a backhoe shovel. I opened my eyes and stared into the face of my father as he carried me to my bedroom.

> "Sing to the Lord a new song, for he has done marvelous things; his right hand and his holy arm have worked salvation for him." (Psalm 98:1)

There's something about Daddy's arms that cannot even compare to a mother's. Soldiers on the battle field cry out for Mother when in pain and rightly so, but Daddy's arms keep away the nightmares. Daddy's arms are the shields of the Gods. Daddy's arms defeat any villain and provide protection.

> "It was not by their sword that they won the land, nor did their arm bring them victory; it was your right hand, your arm, and the light of your face, for you loved them." (Psalm 44:3)

My father has been dead for nearly eight years. But as I write these words, I reflect on his arms. They were not muscled like a body builder's, but they were firm and strong. He had a US Marine emblem tattooed on his right forearm. When I was just a child, the globe, anchor, and eagle were clear and distinct. However, as he aged, the ink blurred.

By his death at age eighty-four, my dad's arms had encountered life at its best and and its worst. They lived through the Great Depression when he was a lad. They embraced his mother in grief when two of his siblings passed on in their youth. This was common back in the early 20th century. I believe the mortality rate of young children was one of the reasons for large families.

My dad didn't participate in organized school sports but his father put him to work in his gas station and mechanic shop. There were no machines for assisting in changing tires when he was a teen. Muscle, sweat, busted knuckles, and strength were the four key ingredients in repairing a flat. The summer before my dad entered the US Marines, he 'plowed a mule' as he put it. There were no tractors on the *Goree Place*. So just like the pioneers of old, my dad pushed, sweated, cussed, and followed the south end of a north-bound mule for a whole summer.

I will never know all of what my dad's arms experienced in the Marines—he never spoke of his terror on Saipan and Tinian, but I've tried to imagine. After his death, I turned my grief into studying every book I could find about the Marines during their Pacific conquests of islands annexed by the Imperial Japanese Army. I started with the invasion of Tarawa, and completed my research with the taking of Okinawa in 1945. Most of my reading came from authors of my father's generation, men who wrote anywhere from five to thirty-five years later about their personal experiences. Believe me, the battles were brutal. I have somewhere between 300 to 400 books in my growing private collection.

My father's arms experienced eight weeks of boot camp in San Diego, California. Due to America's need for troops, training was shorter back then. His arms strained during push ups, jumping jacks, using pongee sticks and bayonets. They were bruised and bleeding from obstacle courses and hand-to-hand combat. Those arms also grew stronger from digging six-foot holes deep into the sand to bury a cigarette butt. Then covering it up with sand, but ordered immediately to unbury it so the drill instructor would not have litter where he trained his men.

My father was in the Fourth Amphibious Division where he trained to drive an LVT, (Landing Vehicle Tracked), amphibious vehicles designing to transport troops or supplies. I know from my research he had to have strong arms to hold the steering wheel in place to keep the vessel heading toward the shore. Although I don't know which beach landing site he was assigned, I do know what may have frightened him and weakened his arms.

Although I could state the size and caliber of the shells the Japanese fired at him and thousands of other Marines, their size would mean nothing to the casual reader. Let's just say, on the way to the shore my dad's arms held fast as he looked to his left and saw a vehicle just like his disappear with all hands lost. By this

I mean man, motor, and machine vaporized by a direct hit. Perhaps he looked to the right and saw a near-direct hit and watched as another LVT like his fly up in the air fifteen feet and break apart. This time he saw legs, arms, heads, and torsos spew in different directions. Yet my Dad's arms held firm on the wheel, guiding his vehicle to the shore.

> "My hand will sustain him; surely my arm will strengthen him. No enemy will subject him to tribute; no wicked man will oppress him. I will crush his foes before him and strike down his adversaries. My faithful love will be with him, and through my name his horn will be exalted." (Psalm 89:21–24)

I could tell you much more but details of my father's story are not the point of this writing. After the war ended, my dad left the Marines and spent the rest of his life raising my brother and me. He was married to my mother for seventeen years, but they divorced and he remarried. He spent forty-five years with my stepmother before passing on to his reward. All through his lifetime, no matter how tired his arms were, they were always there for his children.

What is my point of this brief biography? I want to make two comparisons.

First, God's arms are there to support us, follow us, and lead us. God's arms can be seen in my father's dependable and enduring arms. Just like when I was a kid with my dad, my heavenly Father lifts me up on his shoulders to see the world from a holy perspective. I felt like a king when sitting on my Dad's shoulders, a perch which allowed me to see far into the distance, a viewpoint I could have never had on the ground. He either held onto my legs or put one arm around to the small of my back to hold me tightly. When I was on his shoulders I was never fearful, but felt powerful!

Do you not think this is exactly what God's arms do for us? Is he not there when we pray, setting us high on his shoulders so we can see distant futures? Does he not hold us safely on his shoulders so that we feel like kings?

"Blessed and holy are those who have part in the first resurrection. The second death has no power over them, but they will be priests of God and of Christ and will reign with him for a thousand years." (Revelation 20:6)

Second, God's arms never grow tired, unlike my father's arms. God's arms were not created, nor are they subject to human growth and maturity. They didn't start out as a fetus in a womb, experience birth, and then encounter life as a human. This was reserved for his Son through whom he worked his will on this earth. Our heavenly father's arms didn't begin as a young boy's, grow into a man's, then later in life, hit a peak in male strength, and atrophy in old age.

"Since the children have flesh and blood, he too shared in their humanity so that by his death he might destroy him who holds the power of death—that is the devil— and free those who all their lives were held in slavery by their fear of death. For surely it is not angels he helps, but Abraham's descendants. For this reason he had to be made like his brothers in every way, in order that he might become a merciful and faithful high priest in service to God, and that he might make atonement for the sins of the people. Because he himself suffered when he was tempted, he is able to help those who are being tempted. (Hebrews 2:14–18)

God's arms hold his creation together. What we know as the universe and beyond are but a speck within the embrace of his all powerful arms. And if this grand cosmos is but a pinpoint, what else lays within the grasp of his arms? What else has he made and held together or plans to make and hold together with his arms? Our finite minds insult God by thinking what he can hold in his arms is only the universe as we know it.

"Ah, Sovereign Lord, you have made the heavens and the earth by your great power and outstretched arm. Nothing is too hard for you." (Jeremiah 32:17)

Coming down from the lofty theological thoughts about God beyond the universe, how does his embrace, through Jesus's arms, impact us on earth?

I believe there are six ways.

First, his arms embrace our grief.

Some time back, a young man in his early forties came to my office for counseling. When we first met several months previously, Mike reminded me of Hercules. Not only was he a big, handsome youth, but sharp, educated, and articulate. During our visits, he shared that his marriage was in a meltdown. Well at this visit, Mike reported his situation had not improved. His wife had made some changes in the way she treated him, but he had lived too many years in pain due to her emotional neglect and abuse. Seems she'd been in an abusive relationship before marrying Mike, and she exploited his kind nature to her advantage. It was apparent that she was punishing him for her first husband's mistreatment. She knew she'd suffer no reprisal from him for her neglect and abuse because, for although he had a Herculean physique, he was a marshmallow on the inside.

During our hour conversation, Mike tried to hold back his tears while we discussed his situation and developed a plan for him to follow. When it was time to leave I could tell he needed a hug, so I suggested he let me embrace him as my own son—who was a US Marine at the time. That invitation was all he needed. I wrapped my arms around him and held him as tight as I would my son. And this *big boy* grabbed me like a gorilla! I thought he was going to break my back. But he needed a *daddy* that afternoon, a father to tell him he would get through this trial. Mike needed me, not as his counselor, but as a gray-haired father-figure, to hear me tell him he was loved and cared for like my boy. This perfectly natural father and son embrace is what God does with us.

Second, his arms tell us we can.

I'll use my interactions with another client to illustrate this point. Robert was a young man, as gentle as a lamb. But during my first session with him and Anna, his wife, I could tell he had suffered terrible abuse as a child. After we'd had several more sessions, I realized the abuse I suspected only touched the hem of the garment of his mother's pathological torture. All his life, Robert was told by his alcoholic mother that he would never succeed in anything. He was told don't try that sport because you'll only fail. Don't pursue that interest because you'll make a mess of it. And college, don't consider attending college because you won't finish high school.

Guess what happened? He fulfilled his mother's degrading prophecy in every aspect of his life. It didn't take long for him to lose ambition and desire to succeed. His wife's love and support helped turn his life around. Out of school, with no qualifications, he worked an hourly wage job which became a blessing in disguise. Robert met Anna on the job and the two got along famously. She was attracted to his kind, gentle nature, and he was attracted to someone who was not critical. Soon, they fell in love and married. They came to counseling not because of marital problems, but because he was still struggling with his inner sense of failure that prevented him from finding a direction for his life.

I quickly discovered that he would benefit from a basic act of human love. He needed a father figure to tell him, "You can." I repeated the phrase to him over and over, during every counseling session. In no time, he began to believe *he could*. He still had doubts. Erasing two decades of being immersed in a *you can't* atmosphere could not occur over night. But during the months of counseling, he gradually began to build confidence in pursuing the education necessary for a satisfying career.

I believe God's embrace through Jesus is his way of telling us, "You can!" We can accomplish nothing through our own power, but all things are possible through the power God offers in Jesus and his embrace.

Third, his arms offer forgiveness.

Several years ago, a young woman came to my office for counseling. Julia's tale was so tragic she felt she couldn't accept God's forgiveness. The irony of her plight is that like all self-imposed guilt, she blamed herself for an incident that was not due to her negligence. Julia related she was sitting in a chair early one morning, breastfeeding her baby. She was exhausted because she had been up all night. While feeding the baby, she fell into a deep sleep with her baby nestled in her arms. When she awoke she found her baby's face had turned a pale blue. Julia realized that in her sleep her baby's head had been caught between her breasts and he suffocated to death.

Since her husband had already left for the office, she immediately dialed 9-1-1. At the hospital the baby never recovered and was pronounced dead. By this time her husband had joined her in the emergency room. Child Protective Service were involved in the case, but she was not charged with murder.

Julia was never able to get over the death of her child. She still blamed herself, and although they tried to reconcile, the marriage ended in divorce. She began drinking, and partying several times a week, and because she was angry at God, she denounced her faith. Although Julia did not proclaim to be gay, she began practicing homosexual behavior.

She refused to return for counseling and continued her self-destructive lifestyle. Last I heard, she was living with another woman and still running wild. She could have been free of guilt had she accepted that Jesus stood beside her during the tragedy of her baby's death. She could have been healed by Christ's embrace, but she refused to accept his offer.

Forth, his arms heal our abuse.

Teresa, a beautiful, young African American lady, came to my office for counseling. During our initial session, not once did she look me in the eye. She stated she'd been hesitant to attend counseling because she didn't want to confront the years she had endured physical and sexual abuse. Teresa had been abused so often, by men whom she should have been able to trust, she refused to look people in the eye. Somehow over time, this behavior had become her way of avoiding the chance of becoming close to anyone. Why she took a chance on trusting me I don't know to this day. Over the course of time she gradually, but infrequently, began to look me in the eye. During one session, several weeks later, we had a pretty normal interaction, with Teresa engaging in eye contact. Although she had an appointment schedule for the next week, I never heard from her again.

I believe Jesus was beginning to heal her abuse and because his arms were drawing too close, she ran away. Sometimes people become so accustomed to a life of pain that the experience of relief feels unnatural and uncomfortable. Hence, they retreat to what they know best—discomfort. I only pray that at some later time Teresa allowed Jesus's arms to remove her pain.

Fifth, his arms release us from our addiction.

Many years ago I had a contract to conduct psychological evaluations for patients admitted to emergency rooms who presented with severe psychiatric symptoms. Late one night at a hospital ER, I interviewed a malnourished, dehydrated young Hispanic woman. It seems Eva was in her early twenties, had a child less than ten years of age, and was from a border town in Texas. Although she showed academic promise in high school, she chose a life involved with a gang. Soon, she began using heroin and became addicted. Eva's story could have made headlines in the local news—she turned to prostitution and petty theft to support her habit, and had no place to live, except on the streets.

That night, Eva had entered the ER either because she needed a fix, or she wanted help to overcome her addiction. During my assessment interview, she stated she wanted to get clean. I spent several hours pulling strings to get her admitted into a reputable drug rehab facility where her treatment would have been free. All she had to do was wait while the admitting process was completed. Unfortunately, my shift ended before she was admitted. However, before I left, I made her promise she would wait until the hospital was ready to admit her.

A few weeks later, I was assigned another case at the same ER. When I saw the doctor who had evaluated Eva, I asked for an update. He said she'd walked out after I left, and they had not seen her since. I was saddened at the news because Eva had been snatched up by Satan. She'd made yet another decision to abandon the freedom the arms of God could have provided.

Sixth, his arms rejoice with us.

Sometimes I become frustrated when I tell people, "You can," only to discover many of them are fearful of success. Once I had a twenty-five-year-old African American client come to my office for counseling. Martha always had the same complaint—she was miserable in her job. I asked her if she had a pot of gold what would she do. She informed me she wanted to be a pharmacist.

Here's the kicker, as we say in Texas. I replied in a somewhat commanding voice, "Then go become a pharmacist."

She immediately said, "Oh, no, I can't."

"Why not?"

"I have a year-old son, and I have to work."

Then I told her she had her plan all backwards. Instead of thinking she could not become a pharmacist because she had no money, she needed to *decide* to go to school first and then find the money so she could pursue her dream.

Prior to our conversation, Martha had never thought to fulfill her dream in this manner. She had *settled* which is why she was miserable. I told her she had two options. She could either stay where she was and be unhappy, or she could fulfill her dream and realize her greatest potential.

A few weeks later Martha came to tell me she was leaving her job. She'd decided to finish college and apply to pharmacy school. I know the angels in heaven were rejoicing because she was embraced by the arms of God who guided her to success.

6

Hands That Held Creation

What hands are these—rough, gnarled, and calloused,
Covered with scars, excessive as though deliberately inflicted
with cold malice?

Nails torn and splintered, some up to the cuticles' white half-moon.
Pain I know these injuries caused from a hard life ended too soon.

Wood He knew how to shape, mold, and create,
For thirty years a Carpenter of humble origins and
not a self-styled potentate.

But these same strong hands gently nestled an innocent lamb,
Healed the blind, restored sight and hearing to those living without a gram.

With one wave of these hands over ocean and sea,
He calmed storms, changed tides for all mankind to see.

The dead were raised, and shattered relationships were restored,
Yet at thirty-three His hands abruptly experienced a different use
of nail and board.

His blood freely flowed, deeply soaking the rings of a saddened tree,
So that in His sacrifice He brought eternal life for those who believe
in His victory.

"In the absence of any other proof, the thumb alone
would convince me of God's existence." Sir Isaac Newton

Christ's Hands Were There:

After the dreadful Hurricane Katrina hit New Orleans in 2005, I spent two weeks in the city, providing grief counseling for a company's employees. I will never forget the experience. The first sight that grabbed my attention as we left the airport on our way to the city center were the dirty high-water marks on bridges and elevated walkways. They looked as though a giant went wild with his black crayon. Obviously, the marks indicated how high the flood had risen. I could imagine torrents of water raging, like in Noah's flood, trapping people on the high ground while washing others away.

Another unusual sight were the multiple layers of stoves, refrigerators, and other appliances smashed almost flat. They were piled high in rows like so many corpses stricken down in combat. They reminded me of photos I had seen of US Marines in World War II whose bodies were laid on the ground, positioned like cords of wood waiting to be buried.

But these appliances were waiting to be collected and removed to a dump.

These memories of my initial approach to the city of New Orleans still have the power to shroud me in helplessness. Why, you might ask? The heartbreak I feel as I write goes beyond the devastation of a town, and the loss of life and livelihood. Each one of those appliances represented hopes and dreams of a married couple. In the not too distant past, these appliances were in stores, shiny and brand new. Each one caught a young wife's eye and she just had to have it.

She then convinced her husband they could afford to pay it off over time as their credit score was good. Upon the appliance's arrival at their home it became the gemstone of the young wife's kitchen. No telling how many times she had it adjusted, to the detriment of her husband's back. She just had to have it balanced perfectly. Many hours were spent cooking over a stove or filling a refrigerator or freezer with food for the family.

And now here were those same appliances. Hundreds, thousands. Imagine if they could talk. They would tell all kinds of stories, good and bad about the homes in which they once lived.

Now homeless, they were like many of their owners, cast away on catastrophe's heap. Did some of their owners get swept away in the flood, never to be heard from again? Were others perhaps rescued from the tops of their homes? And what about the homes? Were there now only concrete foundation slabs that survived the flood while their structures had been washed away? These were the contemplations about the flood's devastation that plagued my heart. In spite of all the suffering I had seen, I believe God was there.

Christ's Hand is Revealed in What Didn't Happen:

How, you might ask? Christ's hand is seen in what could have happened but didn't. Further, Christ is seen in who was rescued by his hand and never knew it. How many people didn't drown, who would have, had his hand not steadied the ebb and flow of the flood? Were there homes and businesses that Satan had planned to whisk away but Christ's hand stopped him? Remember what was written in the Old Testament about Noah and the flood when God wanted to wipe man away from the earth?

> "So the Lord said, 'I will wipe mankind, whom I have created, from the face of the earth—men and animals, and the creatures that move along the ground, and birds of the air—for I am grieved that I have made them.' But Noah found favor in the eyes of the Lord." (Genesis 6:7–8)

Let's get specific in other considerations. How many helpless babies didn't drown? How many elderly people where not swept away by the storm? How many children, the sick at home, and those in the hospitals never knew they had been slated to die by Satan, but instead God saved them? Did farm animals and pets, which were thought drowned, show up in pastures or on door steps days or weeks later?

Now let's move to another arena where people fail to see the work of Christ. How many couples in the turmoil of divorce proceedings changed their minds after Hurricane Katrina? Could it be the personal threat of the storm made them realize how petty their differences were? Did not this new insight into their relationship cause them to reunite? And finally, did not this awakening from the nightmare of personal selfishness into the consciousness of selflessness lead them to matrimonial stability?

God's insight into what is best for our lives is eternal and therefore not limited to the here and now. Not only can he see into the future, but his vision follows to the end of time and to the beginning of a new heaven and new earth. (Revelation 21:1) Hence, his decisions made for us are based on what he knows is best and not on what *we* think is best for our lives. Having stated this eternal principle, look at the vast shift in population after Hurricane Katrina. Many inhabitants moved away for safety. Some returned, but others remained in the areas where they'd fled and built new lives.

Could it be for the thousands of residents who never returned to New Orleans that what they needed was a catastrophe like Hurricane Katrina? Was Katrina a final push to make a move, to pursue a change, dream, or goal that they otherwise would not have made? Was it the catalyst that brought them to a new awareness? If the hurricane had not come when it did these people may have come to the end of this life never knowing if their dreams were possible? These statements could also be true for those who did return to New Orleans, or for those who stayed and survived the hurricane. Perhaps, starting over with virtually nothing made them realize they had everything to gain and nothing to lose by initiating their dream?

Listen to the words of Isaiah about how God cares for his people.

"So do not fear, for I am with you; do not be dismayed, for I am your God. I will strengthen you and help you; I will uphold you with my righteous right hand." (Isaiah 41:10)

An Aluminum Flag:

One day when I was exploring the hotel where some of the employees I was counseling worked, I entered the kitchen and struck up a conversation with one of the chefs. My goal as an onsite grief counselor was to conduct informal counseling by private conversations in a casual manner.

During our chat, Phillip revealed a very interesting story. He asked me to look through the glass portion of the kitchen's back door and tell him what I saw in the open courtyard. Although I cannot recall every detail, I remember a large, ragged tree, with bare branches, some twisted into grotesque shapes. At its base, tied by a strong rope, was a two-man aluminum fishing boat.

When the hurricane hit, Phil elected not to leave his post in the kitchen. He pointed to the tree and boat now resting in a natural position, and detailed a story beyond imagination. He said the storm began as a whisper, but in no time, it escalated to a fury. At first, the branches of the tree bent and swayed while dust and trash swirled into the courtyard. But then he noticed a spectacular change. The winds quickly increased in speed and the boat began to vibrate which morphed into shaking, and suddenly the boat lifted off the ground like an airplane. Soon the boat flapped in the winds like a flag on a high mast. Phil watched in amazement as the boat lifted higher and higher. Water began to fill the courtyard and the boat continued to flap as though made from cloth.

As a trusted sentry, Phil remained at his post throughout the storm. He couldn't remember exactly how much time passed, but after what seemed an eternity, the torrential winds that lifted the boat to flail like a flag decreased, which allowed the craft to settle back on the ground.

Upon reflection, Phil realized the boat could have caused extensive damage if it had smashed into the door and broken the glass. But it didn't. If the glass had broken, the kitchen would have flooded in a blink. But it didn't. Phil might have been injured, or thrown into the mouth of the storm. But he wasn't.

He manned his station regardless of the odds against his survival. I remember thinking while he related his story that he was either foolish or brave. By the time he finished, I concluded he'd shown bravery to stay. Brave because this was not just his job, but his home and life.

Christ's Hands Have Divine Purpose:

What prevented Phil from being injured or drowned in the storm? Again, I believe the Lord's hand can be seen. Still, I wonder why his hand prevented Phil's death when so many other people were not saved. Weren't there many other residents just as brave? How many other New Orleans citizens also stood their ground, but passed away into oblivion? I don't know the answers to these questions, but this true story illustrates something important about how Christ's hands works. He chooses where and when to extend his hand of mercy, and it's not our place to question, but to accept. God's actions fit into a plan for mankind that only he knows.

> "For I am the Lord, your God, who takes hold of your right hand and says to you, Do not fear; I will help you." (Isaiah 41:13)

The Crater:

One day there was a lull in my routine and one of the employees asked if I would like to tour the city. For several hours, Barbara drove through some of the areas that had suffered the worst damage. If you have seen the movie *Saving Private Ryan*, you will recall the devastation of bombed communities and towns. That was the first image that came to mind as we patrolled some neighborhoods.

Each house we passed had a circle painted on a wall. Most had symbols next to the circle. Barbara explained the civil authorities marked houses they had inspected, and the symbols indicated if bodies were or were not found inside. The code seemed a very practical way of keeping track of life and death.

Upon entering these houses, we saw dark lines at various heights indicating how high the water had reached. To say everything was waterlogged would be an understatement. There were neighborhoods upon neighborhoods, rows upon rows of empty homes, each front door marked with the circle of life or death. Sure, the monetary loss was in the billions, but the higher cost was in the misery of shattered minds, broken hearts, and sorrowful souls.

Additionally, vehicles of all types, models, colors, shapes, and sizes had been pushed around like tiny toys by both hurricane winds and the ensuing flood. At one place the oblivious wall of water had pushed vehicles aside as if they were made of cardboard. But then there was a sight I had never seen and hope never to see again. We drove down one street and in the median were stacks of cars. Now by stacks of cars I don't mean like those in a junk yard, instead there were stacks of vehicles four and five deep and two across, as far as the road extended. It was as if the son of a giant had a temper tantrum and angrily crushed his toys and then stacked them on top of each other.

In the midst of this carnage I vividly remember one, large tree. Throughout our tour, we'd seen many leafless trees littering the ground like casualties of war. Some were split in two, others had snapped at the base, and still others had lost all their limbs and stood like fence post with trunks still in the ground.

But this tree, at least a hundred years old, lay on its side with its root system pulled out of the ground, fully intact. The hole where it once proudly stood was as large as a round, backyard swimming pool, only this one was filled with muddy water. The roots reminded me of the snake head of Medusa of Greek mythology.

As I reflect on our trek through the devastation, I'm still surprised at the thoughts that bombarded my mind. I thought if that tree could talk, what stories could it tell? A seedling when the city of New Orleans was but a dot on a map. It might have lived in a forest and survived fire, wind, and rain. Witnessed life and death as the rule of nature prevailed with predator and prey. Hosted thousands of birds in its branches. Happily, it had seen hatchlings grow to maturity and fly away, and sadly watched as others became prey to predators as they fell from the nest. Who knows, maybe a young man got down on his knee and proposed marriage to his soon-to-be lifelong sweetheart. Maybe another couple enjoyed a picnic lunch fanned by a cool breeze under its branches.

What struck me most was how the tree was pulled out of the earth. It was as though God reached down and gingerly grabbed the tree in his right hand, very close to the ground, and gently tugged the tree out of the earth, making sure he didn't leave any roots behind. Now I want to pose a couple of questions. Why were all the other trees around it literally ripped, torn, and shattered like broken teeth? Have you experienced sitting in a dentist's chair when he pulls a tooth and it breaks in the grip of his surgical instrument? And yet this tree and its intact root system sprawled beside its home. Dozens of other trees, both older and younger, surrounded it in various stages of destruction, so why was this one chosen to lay as though at peace? Maybe God had a purpose for the way the tree was pulled out of the ground.

Was this tree and the hole it left behind any more special than its neighbors? It, too, had the same destiny as the other trees. They would be cut up into smaller logs for burning either in someone's fireplace or in a trash heap. Could it be that this tree had been granted a special reprieve? Had it done something especially good during its centennial? Was the way its life ended a special blessing God granted by his loving right hand? It wasn't that God didn't care for the rest of his wooden children, but maybe this one was special to him.

Christ's Hand Has a Purpose Beyond
Our Understanding:

The image and possible significance of the fallen tree and its perfect hole has driven me crazy. You may not agree with me, but I believe there is a divine plan in the cosmos. There is a purpose for everything, from the microscopic atom, to a flood and storm like Katrina. As I pondered, I asked what I could learn from this perfectly made hole left by the tree God seemed to have pulled out of the earth and set down gently.

First, was there symbolism in the hole? None that I could deduce. Whatever visual I used to gain meaning had to include the tree and the complete root system. Next, I wondered how the way the tree was pulled from its hole fit into the bigger picture of the storm and flood. Still, I could find not an answer.

After more deliberation, the idea occurred to me that the significance was not in the hole, the tree, the root system, or the storm and flood. None of these spectacles of the aftermath of the tragedy had any significance independent from the other. In fact, the entire scenario, the whole event had a spiritual implication, far beyond our understanding. They illustrate that God is our parent and it's not important for us to grasp how his hand is at work in our lives on every occasion. The important fact is that God is in charge and that's all we need to know.

> "'For my thoughts are not your thoughts, neither are your ways my ways,' declares th Lord. 'As the heavens are higher than the earth, so are my ways higher than your ways and my thoughts than your thoughts.'" (Isaiah 55:8–9)

Or, listen to the writer of Ecclesiastes. "As you do not know the path of the wind, or how the body is formed in a mother's womb, so you cannot understand the work of God, the maker of all things." (Ecclesiastes 11:5)

Many times in counseling sessions, people ask why God would let a tragedy occur in their lives. Usually when this sincere question is asked they are referring to a death, loss of job, bankruptcy, or divorce. We can ask this same question for the terrible storm and flood that hit New Orleans. If we look at this special tree as a microcosm and expand its unusual circumstance to the city's overall recovery, we see a plan much bigger than any one person can grasp. Was Katrina terrible? Of course it was. Was there a great deal of suffering? Yes, indeed. But where people make a mistake is they want someone to blame. When in truth there is a step they need to make before seeking answers.

People seek human explanations about events they attribute to the divine. Mired in their pain, they are searching for a solution where there is no solution, because in God's plan there is no problem. Here is the step they need to take. They should separate the explainable from the unexplainable and not lump the two together as one. For example, people drowned because they were under water without air and could not breathe. Property and treasure were lost, overwhelmed by forces of nature they were not structurally engineered to withstand. Looting occurred because law and order was temporarily replaced by survival of the fittest. The infrastructure collapsed because both flood and storm dismantled what man had created.

Here is the explainable. I saw the path part of the flood had taken as it marched forward, erasing houses, trees, and other well-grounded objects. Then, right next to this devastation, houses, trees and other permanent objects were barely touched. How can this phenomenon be explained? Here's a layman's description. The wall broke at its weakest point, allowing the water to gush through. Why did the wall succumb at that particular point? Perhaps the materials used were inferior, or the construction was faulty, or just the right pressure at the right time caused the break. I'm no engineer so I really don't know. I'm just speculating.

Here's the unexplainable. I talked with a woman whose home was unscathed, but houses around hers were destroyed. I'm sure her story is not the only one of this nature. Another woman related that prior to the storm, she went out of state to visit relatives while her husband remained in their New Orleans home. She tried to get him to leave, but he refused. When she returned, her house and her husband were gone.

Why did she just happen to be out of state when this happened? Why did her husband die, and Phil, the chef, survive? I'm sure there are hundreds of stories where people were rescued just in time while others in similar circumstances perished.

The explainable events can be answered by science, technology, meteorology, and physics. But what about the stories where there is no explanation? Did some people die and others survive by pure chance? No. The answer is found in a Creator who fashioned the world in which we live and then created the laws by which it functions. When those laws are not respected then man suffers the consequences. But there is another set of laws. These laws are only known by God, and they allow his Son's hands to offer mercy to those he chooses. In our finite minds we don't understand the logic because the finite will never grasp the infinite.

Our finite grasp of reality is similar to the flea on the back of an elephant. To the flea, the elephant is his universe. Until one day when the elephant decides to take a bath in a river and spews water on his back where the flea lives. Then suddenly, the flea's world is unraveled. He had no knowledge of how large the world was until he went sailing off the elephant's back into the river.

Humans are like this flea. We have no knowledge of how much bigger our universe could be. In our arrogance, we think we have all the answers. What's going to happen when one day we are washed off our universe and splash into a river beyond our perception?

> "We can land men on the moon, but, for all our mechanical and electronic wizardry, we cannot reproduce an artificial fore-finger that can feel as well as beckon."
> John Napier

7

Feet That Crossed the Milky Way

Our Lord had dirty, smelly feet,
Because He walked to every little town and county seat.

Those feet were constantly calloused, aching and sore,
For they carried the heavy problems only He bore.

These worries were not of flesh and bone's earthly weight,
But of the magnitude of how to usher all through heaven's gate.

Often bleeding, while proceeding with one foot before the other,
There was always one more mile, one more soul He called brother.

Then after three years of aching muscles and bone-wrenching pain,
Not rewarded, but crucified, these feet received nails for their gain.

To His enemies, this defeat was in truth victory for His followers,
don't you see,
Because His blood-soaked feet gave His believers life for all eternity.

When our granddaughter was little, she often spent time with us. One afternoon while my wife and I entertained her on the back porch, our dog dashed across our property to the fence at the far end. Before we could react, our little princess jumped down the stairs and took off after the dog. Now Xaia loved to go barefoot. My wife noticed the four-year-old's shoes and socks beside a chair, and hollered for her to return.

But on this bright, sunny day, Xaia tore across the cleared acres, unaware of the dangers.

The amazing oddity of her Olympic run was that our property is full of small, sharp rocks, briars, stickers, and patches of field grass and dirt. In her gazelle-like run, she paid no attention to her delicate feet.

No matter how loudly my wife called out a warning, Xaia was hopelessly lost in her flight. She'd been magically transported into a dance with Mother Nature.

Unbelievable, when she did return to the porch, she had no stickers in her feet or scratches from her jaunt through the rough terrain. Maybe her penchant for going barefoot paid off.

I remember as a boy growing up in Houston during the 50s and 60s that shoes and socks were optional every summer. My friends and I bared our feet every chance we got. It usually took a few weeks for our feet to develop thick calluses, but once the bottoms of our feet were toughened, there was almost nothing on which we could not walk or run. We roamed along the banks of a spring for several miles, as if we were explorers searching for the bayou's origin. If our mothers had known where we were and what we were doing, they would have grounded us for life.

When my wife and I lived in Central Africa and visited among the tribes with whom we worked, we discovered that their feet were as tough as cow leather. If the people wore shoes, they were usually old, of the wrong size, or held together with tape. But then there were the more traditional tribal men and women who rarely if ever wore shoes. Their soles were like rawhide.

Leonardo da Vinci wrote copious notes on his studies of the human form. One of his famous sayings concerns our feet. "The human foot is a masterpiece of engineering and work of art."

Do you know that the human foot contains twenty-six bones, thirty-three joints, more than one hundred tendons, muscles, and ligaments, and a whopping 250,000 sweat glands? These twenty-six bones are about a quarter of all the bones in the human body. Imagine that.

My Podiatrist has an artistic panorama of the human foot on the wall of one of his examination rooms. These feet are displayed in full color exhibiting their genius in purpose, versatility, and durability. God's intricate plan is demonstrated by the structure and design of our feet to enable them to carry the weight of our human bodies.

Feet have become metaphors in language. We talk about hasty feet, quick feet, fast feet, weak, sturdy, and slow feet. Then we use the phrase *he is dragging his feet* when a person is not emotionally invested in something and delays a decision. Feet also *run for the hills* when their owners have done something unacceptable and they are seeking refuge from the law. We can also be *dead on our feet* when we're extremely tired.

Interestingly, you will notice that in most cultures, regardless of race, creed, or religion, any action associated with the human foot or feet is considered degrading. A person's position in society can be determined by what his or her duty entails. The British nobility had footmen who performed menial tasks. In the Jewish society of old, the lowest servant in rank in a well-to-do household washed visitors' feet. Kissing a person's foot or grabbing a person's foot and placing your head on it was a sign of submission. During war, the single goal of a soldier was to put his boot across the face, throat, chest, or back of his enemy. This brutal and humiliating gesture signified victory.

Path, Walk, and Step:

In the book of Proverbs, Solomon writes about man's feet in terms of a path, walk, or step. Man can choose with whom to walk—either God or Satan. Solomon refers to our metaphorical steps as a highway. "The highway of the upright avoids evil; he who guards his way guards his life." (Proverbs 16:17) You might be interested to know there are at least twenty-two verses in Proverbs teaching how a wise man should guide his feet.

Now, I need your imagination while I pose questions and thoughts. How does a god, our God, who lives in spirit and not in flesh, *take a walk* or *stretch his legs*? Obviously, I don't mean these statements literally as God picking up a piece of concrete or having his body stretched on a medieval torture rack.

In Genesis 3:8 we read, "Then the man and his wife heard the *sound of the Lord God* as he was *walking* in the garden in the cool of the day, and they hid from the Lord God among the trees of the garden." (Italics are the writer's.)

Evidently, Adam and Eve were accustomed to *walking* with God in the Garden during the cool, late afternoons at sunset. We are not told how often this happened or if it was a routine or at random. This passage is the only reference of God walking with his male and female creation.

At this point in Genesis, the walk occurs during an unhappy chapter for Adam and Eve. They had eaten the forbidden fruit and were trying to hide from God. I am not going to explore the topic as it is not the point of this book. Let's proceed to what is meant by God walking.

Since God is spirit, it's obvious that Adam and Eve didn't hear actual footsteps. The Hebrew word for *walking* used in reference to God, literally translated means wind, strong wind, or even storm. Many scholars believe that the writer of Genesis compared the Creator walking to a powerful wind or storm containing God's Spirit that came through the Garden as opposed to the natural breeze that usually passed through Eden. This event preceded their conversation when he asked them why they were hiding. So we know from this passage God has walked with his creation at earlier times. However, God walking doesn't entail the same concept we associate with the action.

And yet, we are told in Genesis 1:26–27, "Then God said, 'Let us make man in our image, in our likeness, and let them rule over the fish of the sea and the birds of the air, over the livestock, over all the earth, and over all the creatures that move along the ground.' So God created man in his own image, in the image of God he created him; male and female he created them."

Does this mean there's a contradiction between these verses and Genesis 3:8? Biblical scholars disagree on the meaning in these verses.

At this point, I'd like you to sit back and use your imagination. What is God like? What does he do when he is not busy with man? What makes us think we are the center of his universe even if he existed in time as we do? Before the Triune created the universe, what existed? Think about this question for a moment. Now ask yourself how long in time did this pre-universe exist? What went on in this pre-world? Did it have a beginning? Since God is infinite and eternal, what is his world like?

Here is another problem. How can we ask what happened in this pre-universe when in truth this question may not be the accurate question at all? Why would we suppose there was activity as we know activity before the Triune decided to create man? Can we finite mortals grasp what the infinite Triune does with their time, when they don't exist in time? How presumptuous of us to ask. If the Triune were to answer these questions would their answers be beyond our understanding?

I am curious about the what, where, and why of events surrounding God in his realm outside of time. What compelled him to create us at that time, other than his love for us as a parent who loves his children? Why create us at all? Are my questions impertinent? Again, even if God were to explain, would I understand? What was his purpose in our creation? Why put us through the misery of life on this earth? More importantly, why create the whole plan of redemption? Could he have not created a better plan so that one of the Triune—his son—didn't have to experience an excruciating death on the cross? I'm sure if I were Jesus, I would have said to God the father, "I'm not going down there. They made the mess, let them clean it up."

Via the big circle of reasoning, these questions return us to Christ's feet. He didn't have appendages before he came to earth, but he knew what they were like. He knew they would be formed in Mary's womb by the Holy Spirit and would then grow like feet of any other fetus. Once born in human form, he knew he'd have toe nails, get splinters, suffer cuts and bruises. Develop corns and calluses, and the bottom of his feet would become as tough as leather. As his feet and legs grew, he'd learn to walk, then run, jump, climb, and stomp in mud puddles. He'd play games with playmates, help his father Joseph and mother Mary, and kneel in prayer.

But what fascinates me the most is that these same feet, before they were human feet, knew no time, no space, no confinement in dimensions, no beginning or end, no pain or any other conditions we humans experience. If he had feet before he volunteered to be born of an earthbound woman, I'm sure they didn't look like any human's feet.

Here is another truth—his feet where his own creation. He made them himself. How many people can say they created their own feet? Scientists and technicians have created robotic forms. Guess whose design their metal contraptions follow? Jesus's.

One last point about Christ's creation of his own feet. While on earth, he didn't have to suffer pain of any type, at no time during his life, especially on the cross. But he chose to accept human pain, in every part of his body so he would know what we as humans experience. How great is that.

Jesus Was the Only Human with Real Feet:

In Greek history there are depictions of Atlas in a stooped position with the earth balanced on his back and shoulders, a comforting picture to assure all who dwell on the planet will be safe and secure. Notice that his upper torso supports the earth, but it in turn is supported by his feet. So you can conclude that the weight of the world rested on his feet. He was the only god given the momentous task to hold the world safely.

The story of Atlas is Greek myth, meaning it's only a story holding no real objective truth. But think of this next historically accurate story from two thousand years ago. Jesus Christ was a real flesh-and-blood Jewish man who lived on earth for about thirty-three years. Both Biblical and extra-Biblical historical documentation confirm his brief life. His crucifixion is also a historically documented fact supported by eye witness testimonies. The manner of Jesus's death is carefully recorded by the Gospel writers of the New Testament, and is also alluded to by secular historians.

The cross rested on Jesus's back which was supported by his feet as he trudged through the streets of Jerusalem to Golgotha, the hill on which he was crucified. So you can also say that the weight of the world's sins rested on our Savior's feet. Only Jesus possessed the feet on which the sins of the world could rest. His feet supported redemption's plan for man—past, present, and future. No other man or god was equipped to accomplish this deed. His feet were unique and exclusive because they were divine.

This is why I say only Jesus had real feet. All other human feet are duplicates. The ultimate designer, our creator, placed Jesus's feet, along with all his other body parts, in Mary's womb through the Holy Spirit. Whereas men's feet are created by flesh and blood through human procreation, copies of the original. Jesus's feet were the only ones strong enough to carry the burden of sin. No man's feet could have carried that enormous weight.

Now think of Christ's sacrifice. Throughout the centuries, there were many men who were crucified, but only one was the Savior. When the Roman soldiers hammered nails into his feet, they had no idea how their actions were fulfilling God's plan. They thought Jesus was just another fool prophet whose fifteen minutes of fame had run its course. When the soldiers spilled his blood by piercing his feet with nails, they were opening up the royal door of divine forgiveness, mercy, and freedom. They had no idea that they were hammering nails into the feet of the one true God. Sure he bled, but his blood was not only human, it was noble. Unlike the royals of this earth, Jesus's blood flowed from the heavenly King of Kings, as foretold by the prophets of Israel.

> "But Christ has indeed been raised from the dead, the first fruits of those who have fallen asleep. For since death came through a man, the resurrection of the dead comes also through a man. For as in Adam all die, so in Christ

all will be made alive. But each in his own turn: Christ, the first fruits; then, when he comes, those who belong to him. Then the end will come, when he hands over the kingdom to God the Father after he has destroyed all dominion, authority and power. For he must reign until he has put all his enemies under his feet. The last enemy to be destroyed is death. For he 'has put everything under his feet.' Now when it says that 'everything' has been put under him, it is clear that this does not include God himself, who put everything under Christ. When he has done this, then the Son himself will be made subject to him who put everything under him, so that God may be all in all." (I Corinthians 15:20–28)

What about after the resurrection when Jesus spent time in various parts of Judea talking to his followers? We don't know how many people were like Doubting Thomas. Only one account with the Apostle Thomas is recorded during the forty days Jesus walked on the earth before his ascension. Thomas would not believe unless he could put his hand in Christ's side. I would have asked for one more sign—I'd want to look at his feet. Sure, we've all hobbled along with blisters hampering our trek, or endured a splinter or two. But those impediments are nothing like having a gaping, ragged hole in each foot! Think of all the bones, muscles, and tendons crushed by the nails. But we are told Jesus walked everywhere he went without hindrance.

> "For what I received I passed on to you as of first importance: that Christ died for our sins according to the Scriptures, that he was buried, that he was raised on the third day according to the Scriptures, and that he appeared to Peter, and then to the Twelve. After that, he appeared to more than five hundred of the brothers at the same time, most of whom are still living, though some have fallen asleep. Then he appeared to James, then to all the apostles, and last of all he appeared to me also, as to one abnormally born." (I Corinthians 15:3–7)

Don't you know there must have been other followers who may have recognized Jesus but still demanded proof? All Jesus had to do was open his garment to reveal his back where the flesh had been torn from the bone and muscle. Or show the spear wound in his side, not to mention the holes in his hands and feet. What about the crown of thorns on his head? Surely those barbs left their marks.

Let's return to Jesus's feet. Some scholars argue the nails were hammered into his ankles between the tibia and fibula in order to carry the body's weight. Others surmise the soldiers used one nail per foot, or one nail pierced through both feet crossed at the ankles.

Personally, I'm not interested in the nit-picking details. The fact remains Jesus had nails hammered through his feet, and we won't know the exact point of entry until the resurrection and second coming. I think we will be fascinated to learn many details we haven't even considered.

What a grand event followers of Jesus must have experienced to recognize Jesus and in the course of their conversations with him look down and see the gaping holes in his feet. Remember, they wore open sandals back then. Disciples probably could have seen clean through each foot to the sole of Jesus's sandal. Can you imagine their excitement, maybe mixed with repulsion? I think I would have fallen down at Jesus's feet and worshipped him. This thought brings me to my final point of this chapter.

We Will Have Christ's Feet Without the Holes:

Now this may sound like an unusual sub-heading, but listen to my reason. Jesus died on the cross because only he could carry the weight of our sins. Holes were bored through his feet so we would not have to endure the same wounds in our feet. Jesus's blood was shed from his feet, spilled for our sins which only he could legitimately carry. And in that instant, as he momentarily carried the weight of man's sins past, present, and future, God turned away because he could not come into contact with sin.

"From the sixth hour until the ninth hour darkness came over all the land. About the ninth hour Jesus cried out in a loud voice, 'Eloi, Eloi, lama sabachthani?'—which means, 'My God, my God, why have you forsaken me?'" (Matthew 27:45–47)

Because of Jesus's sacrifice, we will one day have divine feet like our Savior. They will not be flesh and blood with nail holes. They will be perfect like Christ's. We will dance among the stars, superior to any in the Milky Way or any other star system in the universe as we know it. We will be able to walk as Jesus walked before he became flesh, in the same places he walked. And finally, we will walk where he and God walked in whatever realm they lived before time.

"As was the earthly man, so are those who are of the earth; and as is the man from heaven, so also are those who are of heaven. And just as we have borne the likeness of the earthly man, so shall we bear the likeness of the man from heaven. I declare to you, brothers, that flesh and blood cannot inherit the kingdom of God, nor does the perishable inherit the imperishable. Listen, I tell you a mystery: We will not all sleep, but we will all be changed—in a flash, in the twinkling of an eye, at the last trumpet. For the trumpet will sound, the dead will be raised imperishable, and we will be changed. For the perishable must clothe itself with the imperishable, and the mortal with immortality. When the perishable has been clothed with the imperishable, and the mortal with the immorality, then the saying that is written will come true: 'Death has been swallowed up in victory.'

'Where, O death, is your victory?'

'Where, O death, is your sting?'

The sting of death is sin, and the power of sin is the law. But thanks be to God! He gives us the victory through our Lord Jesus Christ." (I Corinthians 15:48–57)

8

A Back That Bore Our Sins

Was His back created for beating with whips,
Or was its strength designed to make sawdust and wood chips?

Did His Father's vision entail strength to carry a wooden cross?
And did God use the carpenter's life to prepare Him
for death's bloody dross?

I think the plan of a simple carpenter's role in life,
Was to prepare a back strong enough to defeat Satan's evil drum and fife.

God used Satan's hate to murder His Son through the Jews,
To turn the tables on Satan so that His Son's death paid man's mortal dues.

For only a lean, powerful back could have been torn to the bone,
And still live to hang on a cross surrounded by a world, yet alone.

Then shout out in victory that His task was done,
And claim through His last breath that over Satan He had won.

The Tree No One Wanted

There was once an enormous seed that seemed to appear out of nowhere. It was so large it looked like a displaced rock in the forest. It was hard, covered in pockmarks, and sported a dirty, brown outer shell. On the morning the odd-shaped seed materialized on the forest floor, it tried to wiggle its way deep into the soil. All the other newborn seeds were normal, small, and soft, with

85

beautiful tan coloring, and resembled spear tips. Not only were they easier on the eye because they looked like seeds, but they were able to burrow into the soil more readily than the misshapen seed.

No matter how intensely the ungainly, rotund seed tried to tunnel itself deep into the soil it could not burrow like the other seeds. One by one his fellow seeds found a home beneath the soil's surface and were quickly nourished by the nutrients and moisture they found. Meanwhile, Outsider, as the seed was nicknamed by the others, was only halfway buried and it seemed he could penetrate no deeper.

The rest of the seeds laughed at him and called him all sorts of degrading names because he was not handsome like they were. His plain and ugly exterior was reason enough for them to ignore him as they talked among themselves. Outsider epitomized the face that would look through a house's window from the street wishing he could join in the fun and games, but knew no one would notice, let alone invite him in.

Finally, after what seemed an eternity, the large seed felt nutrients and moisture soaking into his thick coat even though he couldn't dig any deeper. Like all the other seeds, he began to submerge his roots deep into the soil to lay a foundation for a steady, secure new home.

As the seeds grew, their slim, tender stems shot skyward, beautiful and as smooth as silk. That is, all except our huge, odd-ball seed. By all accounts, he should have produced a thick, strong stem. But no. His stem was as puny as a weed. It was less than half the height of the rest of the seedlings, bent and crinkled.

"What kind of tree are you going to be?" everyone asked.

All the other saplings and their parent trees took bets on whether or not he would survive the winter.

However, several years passed, and all the trees, except the tree no one wanted, had grown to become strong, tall, and study. Their parents were proud. In the dark of the evening, when no humans were around, the entire group of parent trees gossiped and bragged.

"My son will grow up one day to be a fine sturdy beam in a mighty house. He will hold the rest of the roof's weight and carry the load all by himself, for generations."

"That's nothing," another parent tree said. "My son will grow up to be the crossbeam over a mighty door in the governor's home. He will be so thick and solid those humans will abandon the use of the stone arch and use him alone."

"You two have nothing on *my* son. He will grow up so straight and tall he will be used as a mast on a Roman ship. He will tower above all other masts on the lead ship in the Roman Navy. He will travel the world and have tales to tell no one else around here has ever heard."

Finally, not to be out done, another mother and father tree spoke up and said, "Our son will be a mighty warrior. He will be made into the long beam of a catapult and will hurl massive stones thousands of feet to break down the walls of cities the Romans conquer."

Amidst all this chatter expressing ego, pride, and parental vanity, nothing was heard from the parents of the tree no one wanted. Seems they were the only two of their kind, and none of the other trees had seen where they came from either. As far at the forest inhabitants knew, this was the first time the odd trees had produced an offspring.

Like their seed, the odd parent trees had appeared in the forest unnoticed, grew to maturity, and lived in the shadows, keeping quietly to themselves. They were humble, and stood silently by, listening, not wanting to predict any future for their boy. They were content to let him be part of the forest, and grow to a nice old age, and die from natural causes. Several hundred years of life were reward enough. After all, he would provide shade for humans to enjoy. He could take care of the birds of the air and other forest creatures. And, if necessary, during floods or fires he could use his size to shield small saplings from being washed away or burned.

Many years later, the young trees, including our odd sapling, grew to maturity. No, he was not as big and handsome as the other trees, but he finally filled out and was content with the way he was made. He had already been helping humans and forest animals just like his parents predicted. Satisfied with his place, he felt no inner desire to become anything different. All the other trees continued to ridicule him by saying he had no ambition or desire to improve his lot in life.

Then, one spring day, a bevy of humans approached bearing axes and saws, and riding in large wagons. Now the time of reckoning had arrived. All the young, handsome trees wanted to shout, "Pick me! Pick me!" But they couldn't, so they had to wait and let their size do their talking. Sure enough, each tree of the elite group was chosen, chopped down, and stacked in the wagons to be carted back to Jerusalem.

Just when the men were about to leave, one turned and stood in front of the tree no one wanted. Hands on his axe, he said, "What a strange looking tree. Let's cut it down anyway."

The men completed the task and added the tree no one wanted to the last wagonload. The other trees already in the wagon were indignant. They said amongst themselves, "How dare these humans mix us with that useless stick?"

However, since they couldn't inform the humans of their social blunder, the trees remained silent. The tree no one wanted didn't care about what they said. He was sad because he would not live out his life in the forest. But he had an inkling that being cut down and moved to Jerusalem would provide an adventure he hadn't anticipated.

When the wagons arrived in Jerusalem, the lumbermen displayed the wood for discerning carpenters.

One said, "I'll take this tree to became a crossbeam in a mighty house."

"And I want this one for the beam over a door in the ruler's home," said the second carpenter.

"This extra tall tree will become a mighty mast on a ship I'm building for the Roman Navy." The proud builder pounded his chest.

Not to be outdone, the last carpenter stood next to a fine-looking tree and said, "I have plans for this specimen. It will be perfect for the long beam for a catapult."

As the parent trees predicted, each of their handsome offspring became the wooden fixtures in the human world they had wanted.

What about the tree no one wanted? Ridicule was added to insult. It wasn't enough for each tree to be taken for a magnificent human endeavor, but they each jeered and cursed the tree no one wanted as they left.

"Hey, sap," said one. "That's all you're good for."

"Why don't you turn over a new leaf? Oh, that's right, now that you've been cut down you can't grow any new leaves."

"Hey my man, I think you're barking up the wrong tree. You're nothing like us. You're not in the same class."

But the tree no one wanted ignored their hurtful remarks and was content to be left in the carpenter's storage area where the man stowed fresh-cut wood from the forest. After all, what else could the tree do?

It seemed no human had any grand or noble tasks in store for him. In fact, one day he heard a few carpenters questioning why the logger had bothered to cut down the tree.

Many months later, the humans still had no use for the tree no one wanted. Used to criticism and ugly words, he still cringed every time a carpenter entered the storage area. The morning one mentioned using the tree for firewood was the worst day of his life.

After thinking about his eventual end, he saw a brief silver lining and accepted that even if he was turned into firewood, at least his flames would keep humans warm and cook their food. He would still be serving humans, and he was pleased.

Then one day, lo and behold, the tree no one wanted was selected and taken to a carpenter's shop. He was cut into two thick beams, one shorter than the other. A soldier in uniform collected the shorter beam, splintery and roughly cut, and took it to a place where a man was being whipped.

The tree no one wanted could hardly believe his eyes. Only man used barbed whips to tear away his fellow man's bark right down to the inner rings. So cruel. When the beam noticed all the red sap pouring from the man's back, he was sure the victim was going to die.

Then Roman soldiers angrily grabbed the man from the pool of his red sap spreading on the stone portico, and in the next instant, heaved the beam of the tree no one wanted across the doomed man's shoulders. His red sap soaked into the tree's wood fibers. Dismay showered over the tree no one wanted as his position forced him to rub against the convicted man's flesh. The beam wailed when soldiers whipped the man over and over. While lashing the convicted man, the Romans commanded him to walk. But how could he? After all, his roots, or what humans called legs, were cut and bleeding. And his branches, what humans called arms, were also covered in oozing slash marks. Guilt overwhelmed the tree no one wanted. How could he justify being carried by a human so near death?

The tree no one wanted decided to break an ancient law that harked back to creation, to the brotherhood of trees. He resolved to speak on behalf of the condemned man. After all, with the crowd's shouting and cursing, and a few resolute men demanding the man's release, the tree's voice would not be distinguishable. So shout he did as loud as he could, and although his words of condemnation did indeed blend in with the human crowd, they had no influence over the soldiers.

Midst the commotion, the beam pondered the situation again. Why did so many people hate this man? Why did so few ask for his release? What could this human have possibly done to generate so much violence and evil?

In order for trees to survive from season to season, they have to be sensitive to the world around them. Hence, the tree no one wanted could feel in his rings, all the way to his core that this mob encompassed more than civil unrest. He hated the fact he was forced to be an unwilling participant in the violence, but he realized there was more at stake than this human's untimely death.

Suddenly, a power larger than nature overwhelmed him, filling him with the knowledge that he had a part to play in this human's life. Although he didn't want to admit it, his fate was sealed by a destiny beyond this world.

Wincing, the shorter beam from the tree no one wanted bobbed up and down on the convicted man's shoulders as he staggered through the streets dragging one leg after the other. The beam looked backward and saw a trail of the human's red sap. How could people be so hideously malicious? Many spat on the man, while some hurled rocks and rotten vegetables. Trees would never do this to their kith and kin.

On and on they slogged through the riotous crowd. The beam held back his tears and tried to make himself lighter. How he wished he could relieve the man of his burden completely. He strained to see over the mob. Where were the soldiers taking this convicted human being?

In the meantime, the longer beam of the tree no one wanted had been hauled to the top of a hill that looked like a skull. He watched as Roman soldiers dug a hole and then spread out two sections of rope and four iron nails. The nails were rusty, dirty, and oh, so thick. What were the men doing exactly? The longer beam shrugged. Maybe he'd discover their intent soon. Even though the beam lay on the ground near the hole, he'd been placed at just the right angle on the hill so he could see an angry crowd of humans climbing up the trail.

Squinting, he studied the mob. Was that the other half of himself across the red-sap covered shoulders of a human? By the sneering and jeering sounds, the longer beam determined the man to be a criminal. What part was his other half to play in the condemned man's future?

Just then, the crowd parted. The convicted man could barely stand. His head bowed, his knees buckled and he fell to the rocky ground. The longer beam flinched as his other half fell, too.

The full weight of the shorter beam of the tree no one wanted crashed down on the man's back and shoulders. The beam wanted to sob but the crowd had diminished and he dare not utter a word.

"What's happening now?" the shorter beam silently asked as soldiers aligned him on the ground.

He didn't have long to wait. The soldiers dragged the convicted man to the beam and shoved him down. Centered on the beam with his arms outstretched, the man did not struggle. Not one bit, not even as nails were pounded through his wrists. The shorter beam of the tree no one wanted recoiled with each pounding of the hammer that drove the nails into both ends of his wooden body.

The convicted man yelled in agony, but not as much as the beam expected. In his youth, he'd heard men scream louder when they accidently scraped themselves against an axe. During their trek through the town and up the hill, the man had tolerated the abuse with a stoicism the beam had never encountered in a human before.

With the convicted man secured to the shorter beam, the soldiers hoisted their burden onto the longer beam. Together once again, the two beams became one. They shared their separate experiences in a blink of an eye. The beams of the tree no one wanted wailed silently as the convicted man screamed while his feet were nailed into the longer beam. Soldiers then used the ropes to hoist up the tree no one wanted, dragged it to the previously dug hole, and stacked rocks at the base to stabilize it.

The tree no one wanted glanced to the left and to the right. By the mob's comments, he knew the men, one on each side on similar beams, were thieves. Many hours passed while the crowd waited for the convicted men to die.

Finally, when the three men were pronounced dead, their bodies were removed from the crosses which were then torn down and piled together to be burned at a later time.

When all the humans were gone, the three crosses felt safe to talk. They all lamented over being used for taking of human lives. In the midst of their sorrow, a Dove flew down and landed on the pile of beams.

She announced, "I have been sent from God who has known you all from the time you were seeds."

"Truly?" asked one cross as the tears of all the trees fell to the ground still soaked with the red sap from the humans.

"I want to know why we were used for such evil?" another cross asked.

"Why have you come to us now?" asked the cross made from the tree no one wanted.

The Dove flapped her wings. "You three were chosen from birth to be here this day. You all came from the same type of tree, unique for what God planned. You may ask what type of tree was used to make the cross that crucified his Son, but no one will ever know the truth. Why? Because there will never be another tree like you again."

"I can understand that," said the tree no one wanted. His sobs began to subside so he could catch his breath and talk more clearly.

"Not me," said another tree. "I wanted to be like all the other trees in the forest."

The third tree poked through the pile. "Hush. Let's hear what the Dove has to say."

"Your births were unusual and your lives were different. God knew the other trees where you lived would make fun of you. It was all part of his plan. You were deliberately created to be uniquely common. God wanted all three of you to be plain and ordinary, almost ugly. You were each chosen for this special purpose."

The trees settled down to hear more from God's messenger.

"One of you was chosen for the thief who defended the Savior, while another was chosen for the thief who cursed and ridiculed the Savior. And finally, the third tree was chosen to be the cross on which the Savior of mankind would die."

No sooner had the Dove expressed these words than the tree no one wanted shouted out, "That was me, wasn't it!"

"Yes." The Dove bowed her head.

"I knew it. As soon as I was placed across the Savior's shoulders, I sensed a divine presence, but at the time I didn't know how to explain it. All day long I was overwhelmed with the knowledge that becoming a cross for a condemned man was only a small act.

Now I understand. He was not just any man. He was the Savior of mankind."

The Dove swept her wing over the tree no one wanted. "You're right. That's why, of the three trees, you were the plainest and the most mocked and scorned in life to prepare you for this day. This is a happy day! A joyous day! It's a day of celebration!"

The tree who no one wanted asked, "How can this be? My human died."

The other two crosses echoed the same sentiment.

Raising her head, the Dove replied, "You are all correct. Your humans died." She pointed to the tree no one wanted. "But your human will rise in three days to conquer death. As the Creator's Son, he came from heaven to die as a sacrifice for man's sins, a sacrifice only he could make."

One of the other trees asked, "What part did my human play?"

"Will my human also rise from the grave?" asked the third tree.

The Dove swayed back and forth as if choosing just the right words. "One of the humans accepted the Savior as his Lord and King, while the other rejected him. I'm sorry to be the one to deliver the news, but this is the way it will be until the end of time. Humans will either accept the Savior or reject him. It's up to each human to make a choice. Didn't you notice this phenomenon among the people at the crucifixion? There were many who received him as Savior, but there were even more who rejected him. As it was today so it will be until the end of time."

Then the tree no one wanted stated, "But I feel so guilty! I was used to kill my human. This is against our tree law."

Nodding, the Dove replied, "I understand your reaction. But remember, you were made common so that you would be viewed by other trees as plain and unpretentious. In the same way, the Savior came from a humble family and lived a simple life. God chooses the meek and ordinary to show his strength."

The tree no one wanted bowed his head and sighed. "That's humbling."

In preparation for leaving, the Dove hopped to the highest beam which was part of the tree no one wanted. "From this day forward until the end of time, you will achieve fame. The symbol of the Cross will become the symbol of the Savior's faith. The Crucifix will provide hope, peace, and comfort to those who seek solace. You won't be remembered as the tree on which the Savior died. You will be celebrated as the Cross that made it possible, through the death of the Son of God, for mankind to have eternal life." She then fluttered her wings, soared into the heavens, and disappeared.

During the night, Roman soldiers trudged up the hill and set fire to the wood that formed the three crosses. Did they know the historical significance of what they were doing?

Quietly, the three trees burned, not completely without company. The Spirit of God hovered over the fire as the cracking embers disintegrated into ashes. If human eyes witnessed what happened next, they may report that the ashes were carried away by the wind. But they'd be in error. The ashes from the three crosses were wafted through the air by the Holy Spirit, spread throughout the earth to broadcast the good news to all of nature that the tree no one wanted brought salvation to humanity through his obedience to God's plan.

9

A Body Sacrificed

"Who has believed our message
and to whom has the arm of the Lord been revealed?
He grew up before him like a tender shoot,
and like a root out of dry ground.
He had no beauty or majesty to attract us to him,
nothing in his appearance that we should desire him.
He was despised and rejected by men,
a man of sorrows, and familiar with suffering.
Like one from whom men hide their faces
he was despised, and we esteemed him not.
Surely he took up our infirmities
and carried our sorrows,
yet we considered him stricken by God,
smitten by him, and afflicted.
But he was pierced for our transgressions,
he was crushed for our iniquities;
the punishment that brought us peace was upon him,
and by his wounds we are healed.
We all, like sheep, have gone astray,
each of us has turned to his own way;
and the Lord has laid on him
the iniquity of us all.
He was oppressed and afflicted,
yet he did not open his mouth;
he was led like a lamb to the slaughter,
and as a sheep before her shearers is silent,
so he did not open his mouth.

By oppression and judgment, he was taken away.
And who can speak of his descendants?
For he was cut off from the land of the living;
for the transgression of my people he was stricken.
He was assigned a grave with the wicked,
and with the rich in his death,
though he had done no violence,
nor was any deceit in his mouth.
Yet it was the Lord's will to crush him and cause him to suffer,
and though the Lord makes his life a guilt offering,
he will see his offspring and prolong his days,
and the will of the Lord will prosper in his hand.
After the suffering of his soul,
he will see the light of life and be satisfied;
by his knowledge my righteous servant will justify many,
and he will bear their iniquities.
Therefore I will give him a portion among the great,
and he will divide the spoils with the strong,
because he poured out his life unto death,
and was numbered with the transgressors.
For he bore the sin of many
and made intercession for the transgressors."
(Isaiah 53)

10

So God Made a Savior

About ten years ago my wife purchased two pairs of blue denim overalls for me. I still have them in my closet although they have holes in select places. However, in my opinion, they are still serviceable. She bought them for me to wear when I use my forty-eight-inch blade John Deere riding lawn mower. We have cleared about four acres on our property and every year come spring, I go down to what I joking call the lower forty to cut the grass. I start with the lawn immediately round our house and then proceed to the rough field grass. The whole procedure can take up to four hours.

I enjoy riding my John Deere although I get really dirty. The air becomes thick with dust and sometimes I have to wear a handkerchief over my mouth and nose. I also wear a long sleeve work shirt to protect my arms against the scrub brush, a wide brimmed hat, and ear phones to drown out the noise of the engine.

At the end of the day, my neck is usually black with dirt. My wife rarely lets me enter the house until I've removed my dirt-caked shoes and grimy socks, and attempted to at least brush the top layer of dust from my clothing.

I receive a great deal of satisfaction when I am done. Before I drive the tractor into its shed, I usually coast along the fence line—about a football field's length from our house—and look up the hill to admire the panoramic view of the finished job. The area once covered in weeds and patches of scrubby grass, is now an even, beautiful expanse. As I stand on the back porch the next morning, I gaze down the slope of the hill toward the fence and feel a tremendous sense of gratification. For a city-slicker like me, it's quite a feat to feel a connection to the land, even if my *farmer* experience is on my mower tractor. Now I understand why a farmer feels a unique sense of pride after he's harvested his crops.

Remember, I believe if Jesus came to the earth today, he would have been a farmer, wearing old blue denim overalls, just like I do when I cut my four acres. His hands would have been callused and his neck streaked with dirt. No matter what color shirt he wore, at the end of he day it would be stained with sweat and dust, and punctured by thorns or sharp sticks. His boots and socks would be caked with mud from the hours he spent walking in his fields.

But most of all, I think at the end of each day while admiring the setting sun, a heavenly sense of accomplishment would surround him. For you see, instead of reaping acres of corn or wheat, he would have harvested thousands of souls for his Father.

I believe the best way to conclude the message of this book is to provide an adaptation of a speech given by the radio broadcaster, Paul Harvey. During the 1978 Future Farmers of America Convention, Mr. Harvey addressed the audience with his speech titled "So God Made a Farmer".

I changed the title of my rendition to "So God Made a Savior".

And on the 8th day, God looked down on his planned paradise and said, "I need a Messiah." So God made a Savior.

God said, "I need someone willing to get up before dawn, walk ten miles on dusty, dark roads full of thieves and robbers, and work all day in the fields of lost souls. Then walk ten more miles in the evening, eat supper before entering a synagogue, and stay past midnight debating the meaning of the Torah with the Rabbis." So God made a Savior.

"I need someone with arms strong enough to work with crude, primitive tools as a carpenter for thirty years, and yet gentle enough to comfort a crying child. Someone to draw in crowds of sick, infirmed, diseased, and dying souls to hillsides where he'll preach the Gospel, then tame cantankerous, hypocritical Pharisees. When he comes home hungry, he'll have to wait for his lunch until Mary and Martha are done arguing over what is more important—waiting tables or sitting at Jesus' feet." So God made a Savior.

God said, "I need someone willing to spend all night in the bow of a boat during a torrential storm and watch his disciples cry in fear, but then not get angry because of their lack of faith. He'll say, 'Maybe next year they'll get it.' I need someone who can raise the dead, restore sight to a blind man using mud made with his spittle. Who can feed five thousand people with five loaves and two fish, command legions of demons to leave a man and enter pigs who run off a cliff. Someone who, come planting time and harvest season, will finish his forty-hour week by Tuesday noon, then, hurting from leg cramps and lower back pain brought on by walking and never riding, put in another seventy-two hours preaching." So God made a Savior.

God had to have someone willing to hurriedly trudge the back roads and steep trails to resurrect a dead girl, and yet find the time to stop in mid-field and ask who touched him as he felt power leave him. Ah, the woman with an issue of blood. So God made a Savior.

God said, "I need someone strong enough to enter the temple, and, when angry at the money changers, toss them and their tables out, yet gentle enough to play with children. Someone who will confront a hypocritical, murderous crowd and stop them from stoning a woman caught in adultery with only a few, well-spoken words. It has to be someone who will confront Satan straight forwardly in his own lies, without reservation. Someone who knows how to seed, weed, and feed the crowds following him, and yet at the same time, have the patience to train twelve vain, selfish, ambitious disciples. A man who at the end of a hard week's work would walk five miles to the synagogue."

"Somebody who'd bale a family together with the soft, strong bonds of sharing, who would laugh, and then sigh, and then reply with smiling eyes, when his son says he wants to spend his life 'doing what dad does.'"

So God made a Savior.